Waltham Forest Libraries

Please return this item by the last date stamped. The loan may be renewed unless required by another customer.

3 0 DEC 2010	3 0 SEP 2014	
- 8 MAR 2012		Wilkins
31/3/13		
13/2/14		

Need to renew your books? **http://libsonline.walthamforest.gov.uk/** or **Dial 0115 929 3388** for Callpoint – our 24/7 automated telephone renewal line. You will need your library card number and your PIN. If you do not know your PIN, contact your local library.

BATTLE *of* BRITAIN

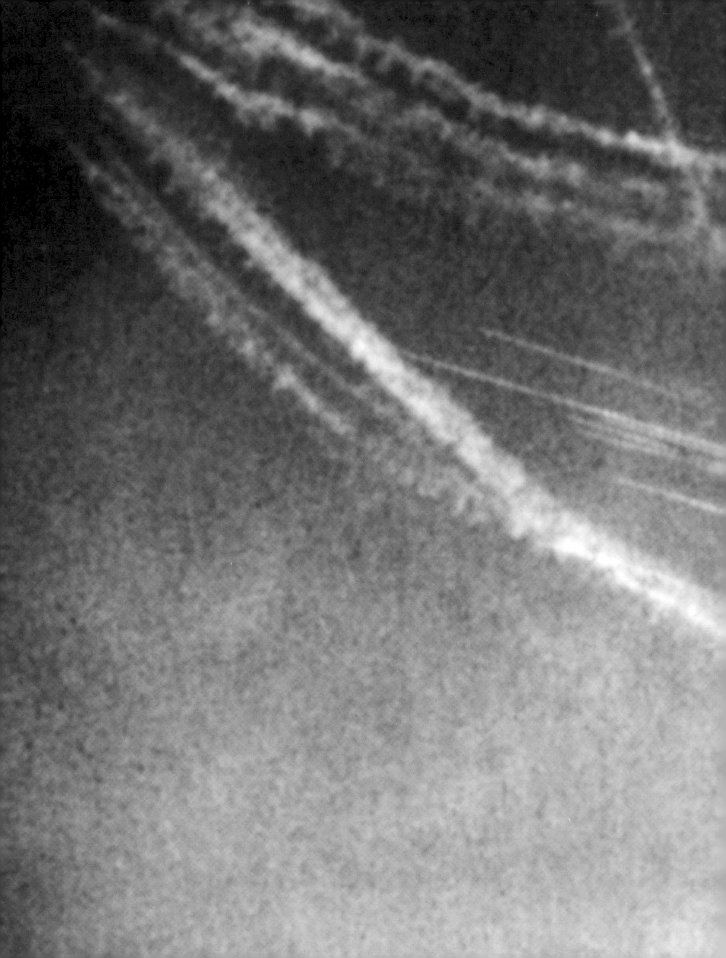

BATTLE *of* BRITAIN

A SUMMER OF RECKONING

Dr. ALFRED PRICE

CLASSIC

An imprint of
Ian Allan Publishing

The Author

Dr Alfred Price served as an aircrew officer in the Royal Air Force where he specialised in target penetration tactics and electronic warfare. He left the service in 1974 and has since worked full-time as an author. He is an acknowledged authority on the history of military aviation, a subject on which he has published more than 30 books and 200 magazine articles.

Author's Note: The correct abbreviations for the Messerschmitt 109 and 110 are, respectively, Bf 109 and Bf 110. However, those abbreviations are not to be found in RAF documents of the World War II period, which use the abbreviations Me 109 or Me 110 throughout. To preserve authenticity, wherever RAF documents are quoted in this book, the Me 109 and Me 110 abbreviations are retained.

Battle of Britain
© Dr. Alfred Price 2010

ISBN 978 1 906537 13 5

Produced by Chevron Publishing Limited
(www.chevronpublishing.co.uk)

© Map: Tim Brown

Published by Ian Allan Publishing
Riverdene Business Park, Molesey Road,
Hersham, Surrey, KT12 4RG

Distributed in the United States of America and Canada by
BookMasters Distribution Services.

Printed in England by Ian Allan Printing Ltd
Riverdene Business Park, Molesey Road,
Hersham, Surrey, KT12 4RG

Mixed Sources
Product group from well-managed
forests, controlled sources and
recycled wood or fibre
www.fsc.org   Cert no. SGS-COC-005526
©1996 Forest Stewardship Council
FSC

…ced or … or by …ernet

Copyright

Illegal copying and selling of publications deprives authors, publishers and booksellers of income, without which there would be no investment in new publications. Unauthorised versions of publications are also likely to be inferior in quality and contain incorrect information. You can help by reporting copyright infringements and acts of piracy to the Publisher or the UK Copyright Service.

CONTENTS

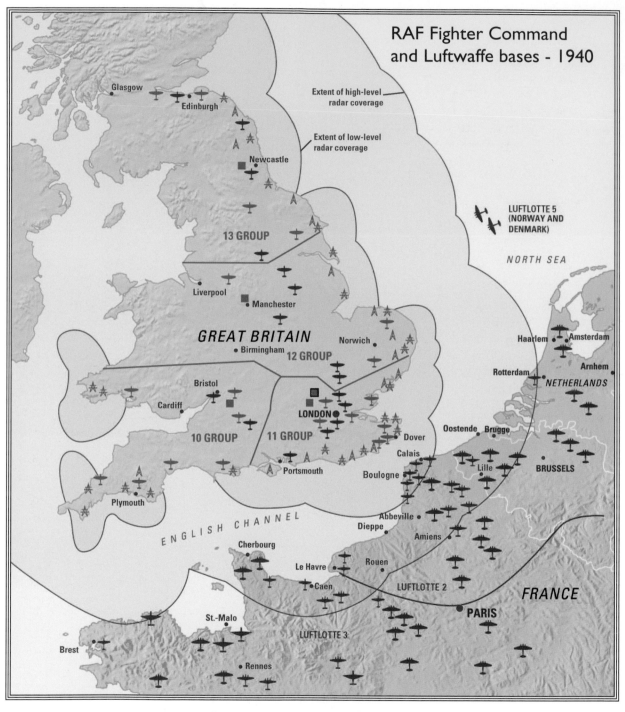

RAF Fighter Command and Luftwaffe bases - 1940

Extent of high-level radar coverage

Extent of low-level radar coverage

LUFTLOTTE 5 (NORWAY AND DENMARK)

NORTH SEA

Glasgow

Edinburgh

Newcastle

13 GROUP

Liverpool

Manchester

GREAT BRITAIN

Birmingham

Norwich

12 GROUP

Bristol

Cardiff

LONDON

Dover

10 GROUP

11 GROUP

Portsmouth

Plymouth

Haarlem

Amsterdam

Arnhem

Rotterdam

NETHERLANDS

Oostende

Brugge

Calais

Lille

BRUSSELS

Boulogne

ENGLISH CHANNEL

Cherbourg

Abbeville

Dieppe

Amiens

LUFTLOTTE 2

Le Havre

Rouen

Caen

St.-Malo

PARIS

FRANCE

LUFTLOTTE 3

Brest

Rennes

KEY

RAF		LUFTWAFFE	
Fighter base		Bf 109 base	
Sector station		Bf 110 base	
Group HQ		Bomber base	
Command HQ		Ju 87 base	
High-level radar			
Low-level radar			

INITIAL SKIRMISHES CHAPTER 1

10 July – 12 August 1940

'Their force is wonderful, great and strong,

yet we pluck their feathers by little and little.'

SIR WILLIAM HOWARD, *OF THE SPANISH ARMADA*

AT the beginning of July 1940 the citizens of the British Isles faced a peril greater than at any time since the despatch of the Spanish Armada in 1588. Seven weeks earlier Adolf Hitler had launched his army in an overwhelmingly successful *Blitzkrieg* campaign in the west that defeated the Dutch, the Belgian and the French armies in rapid succession. The main body of the British army in France had survived only by dint of a brilliantly improvised evacuation from the port of Dunkirk and the beaches to the east.

Now the whole of the European coastline facing Britain, from North Cape in Norway to Biarritz in the south-west of France, was occupied by German troops. Only Great Britain and the Commonwealth remained in the war and few Germans believed she could hold out much longer.

Throughout June and the early part of July the German Government had launched several diplomatic initiatives inviting peace talks. With increasing impatience, the German *Führer*, Adolf Hitler, waited for word that his sole remaining enemy accepted the reality of the situation — that continued resistance was futile. If the British would see sense and make an early settlement, the German dictator reasoned, further bloodshed would be avoided and he could afford to be generous in his demands. But that course of reasoning showed no understanding of the nature of the new British Prime Minister, Winston Churchill. The *Führer* waited in vain.

In a move calculated to bring increased pressure on the British Government, early in July the German leader ordered the *Luftwaffe* to prepare to launch a series of heavy attacks on targets in southern England. He informed his High Command:

'Since England, in spite of her hopeless military situation, shows no signs of being ready to come to an understanding, I have decided to prepare a landing operation against England and, if necessary, to carry it out.'

How the forces compared

Royal Air Force, 1 July 1940

Single-engined fighters	
Spitfires	286
Hurricanes	463
Defiants	37
Twin-engined fighters (Blenheims)	114
Total	**900**

Luftwaffe, 20 July 1940

Aircraft in front line, *Luftflotten* 2, 3 and 5

Fighters:	
Single-engined (Bf 109s)	844
Twin-engined (Bf 110s	250
Bombers	
Single-engined (Ju 87s)	280
Twin-engined (Do 17s, Ju 88s, He 111s)	1330
Long-range reconnaissance	80
Total	**2784**

Air Chief Marshal Sir Hugh Dowding, the Commander-in-Chief of Fighter Command during the Battle of Britain, bore the nicknamed 'Stuffy' and was regarded by his pilots as a cold, aloof figure. Yet he was an exceptionally brilliant and far-sighted innovator, a 'technocrat' before the word had been invented. Dowding's previous post, between 1930 and 1936, had been that of Air Member for Research and Development on the Air Council. The period saw rapid technical changes and his department issued the specifications that had led to the Spitfire, the Hurricane and other types which equipped the RAF during the Battle of Britain. Dowding had also pushed resources into the development of radar and he integrated the new device into his system for controlling fighters. In the history of air warfare, no other commander had played so large a part in the development of the equipment with which his force then went on to fight.

Air Vice-Marshal Keith Park, commander of No 11 Group which bore the brunt of the air fighting over southern England during the summer of 1940. A New Zealander who had flown fighters over France during the First World War, he was a devout Christian who drew great strength from his religion. His air defence fiefdom comprised the whole of south-eastern England, to a line running approximately from Southampton, via Aylesbury, to Lowestoft. Flying his personal Hurricane, Park frequently visited his squadrons to gain a first-hand impression on the progress of the Battle. An energetic and popular leader, Park had the rare gift of being able to make those around him feel that their views mattered.

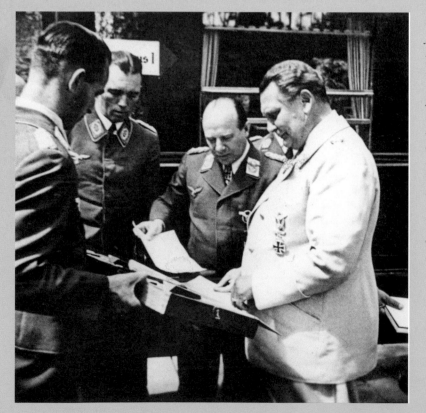

Below: Reichsmarschall Hermann Göring (right) had been Commander-in-Chief of the Luftwaffe since it was formed in 1933. He had been a successful fighter pilot during the First World War, and at the end of that conflict he commanded the famous Jagdgeschwader Richthofen. After the war he played a leading part in the formation of the Nazi Party. By 1940 he was at the height of his political power and had been designated by Hitler as his political successor. Though he is often characterised as a rotund buffoon with a vanity for dressing up, Göring could be both astute and ruthless when the occasion demanded. He is seen here with Ernst Udet to his right and Oberst Josef Schmid, (facing the camera), who was the head of the Luftwaffe Intelligence section.

Generalfeldmarschall Albert Kesselring, was commander of Luftflotte 2 during the Battle. During the First World War he served in the army and rose to become adjutant of a brigade. A capable administrator, he transferred to the new Luftwaffe when it formed in secret in 1933 and became head of that service's Administrative Office.
In the years that followed, he held a succession of progressively more important posts and in the summer of 1940 he had been appointed to command Luftflotte 2. From his headquarters in Brussels he directed Luftwaffe units based in Holland, Belgium and in France as far west as the Seine. A German officer of the old school, Kesselring was firm but courteous to subordinates and greatly respected by them.

Generalfeldmarschall Hugo Sperrle, commander of Luftflotte 3. During the Battle his headquarters was in Paris from which he commanded Luftwaffe units based west of the Seine. During the First World War he had served in the Imperial Flying Service, and transferred to the Army after the conflict. In 1935 he moved to the new Luftwaffe and the following year was appointed to command the Legion Condor, the Luftwaffe contingent sent to fight in the Spanish Civil War. In contrast to Kesselring, Sperrle was an aloof figure and a stickler for protocol. Hitler referred to him as one of his 'most brutal-looking generals.'

Generaloberst Hans-Jurgen Stumpff, commander of Luftflotte 5 based in Norway and Denmark. Following its disastrous intervention in the battle against England on 15 August, this Luftflotte played little further part in the Battle.

The preparations for the landing operation were to be completed by early August, and the role for the *Luftwaffe* was simply stated:

'The English *Luftwaffe* must be so reduced, morally and physically, that it is unable to deliver any significant attack against an invasion across the Channel.'

Yet even by this stage the German leader thought an invasion might be unnecessary. If his air force could deliver a series of sufficiently powerful blows on the enemy homeland he expected that the British, like all of his previous enemies, would come round to his way of thinking.

In July the *Luftwaffe* began a series of small-scale actions over the English Channel, aimed at disrupting British shipping passing through that waterway and forcing the Royal Air Force into battle to defend it. Steadily the air fighting over the Channel became more ferocious, and the Germans began to send 'free-hunting' patrols to engage RAF fighters over southern England.

Hawker Hurricane

The Hawker Hurricane served alongside the Spitfire during the Battle. The most numerous fighter type in service in the Royal Air Force in 1940, the Hurricane equipped thirty-six squadrons and shot down more *Luftwaffe* aircraft than the Spitfire. Carrying the armour and equipment fitted at that time, its maximum speed was 328 mph and the standard armament was eight .303-in machine guns. It was usually detailed to attack the bombers, leaving the Spitfires to tackle the fighters, but nevertheless its excellent low-level manoeuvrability and rugged construction endeared it to its pilots – most of the RAF aces during the Battle flew Hurricanes.

Above: Airworthy Battle of Britain survivor Hurricane Mk I, R4118, was delivered new to 605 (County of Warwick) Squadron at Drem on 17 August 1940. During the Battle it flew 49 sorties from Croydon and shot down five enemy aircraft. After being battle damaged on 22 October 1940, the aircraft was rebuilt and taken on charge by 111 Squadron at Dyce on 18 January 1941.

*The cockpit of Hurricane Mk I
2617 formerly operated by
07 and 615 Squadron on
splay in 607 Sqn markings at
e RAF Museum Hendon,
ondon.*

Typical of the scrappy actions of the period was that on the afternoon of 13 July, when a convoy of freighters passed through the Strait of Dover. Junkers Ju 87s from *Sturzkampfgeschwader* I dived to bomb the ships, and came under attack from eleven Hurricanes of No 56 Squadron. *Major* Josef Fözö, leading a the Bf 109s of 4./JG 51, described what happened next:

'Unfortunately for them [the Hurricanes], they slid into position directly between the Stukas and our close-escort Messerschmitts. We opened fire, and at once three Hurricanes separated from the formation, two dropping and one gliding down to the water smoking heavily. At that instant I saw a Stuka diving in an attempt to reach the French coast. It was chased by a single Hurricane. Behind the Hurricane was a 109, and behind that, a second Hurricane, with all of the fighters firing at the aircraft in front. I saw the dangerous situation and rushed down. There were five aircraft diving in a line towards the water. The Stuka was badly hit and both crewmen wounded, it crashed on the beach near Wissant. The leading Messerschmitt, flown by *Feldwebel* John, shot down the first Hurricane to the water; its right wing appeared above the waves like the dorsal fin of a shark before it sank. My Hurricane dropped like a stone close to the one that John had shot down.'

In that action No 56 Squadron lost two Hurricanes destroyed and two damaged. Two Ju 87s were seriously damaged; JG 51 suffered no loss.

Six days later, on 19 July, nine Defiants of No 141 Squadron were scrambled from Hawkinge to intercept an enemy force approaching one of the convoys. The Defiant, a two-

The Boulton Paul Defiant carried its armament of four .303-in machine guns in the turret amidships and was designed to engage unescorted enemy bomber formations. Its maximum speed was 304 mph, adequate for that task.

Boulton Paul Defiant: The Rationale for the Turret Fighter

During the 1930s there was uncertainty in most air forces concerning the effectiveness of the defensive crossfire produced by a formation of bombers. Would such a crossfire be sufficiently powerful to defeat attacks by single-seat fighters attacking from the rear? It was a matter impossible to prove, one way or the other, in peacetime.

In the RAF the consensus of opinion at the time was that a formation of modern bombers, equipped with powered gun turrets, could probably fight its way through to its targets without suffering heavy losses. But if the bombers' defensive crossfire could be effective in warding off fighter attacks, where would that leave RAF Fighter Command? If its new Hurricane and Spitfire fighters could not engage enemy bomber formations effectively, a major part of Britain's air defence might prove ineffective.

The basis for all RAF calculations in the late 1930s was that the main air threat to Britain would come from *Luftwaffe* attacks mounted from airfields in Germany. In that case, the distances involved meant that the raiders could not be escorted by single-engined fighters. So any method introduced to counter the bomber formations would not suffer from enemy fighter interference.

Enter the turret fighter, the Boulton Paul Defiant, with its armament of four Browning .303-in machine guns mounted in a power-operated turret amidships. The expected scenario was that as it approached the enemy bomber formation a section of three such fighters, or two or three such sections of three, would move to a position to one side and below, or ahead and below, the enemy formation. The aim was to take up a position where the bombers' defensive fire was either weak or non-existent. From there the turret fighters could bring the bombers under withering sustained fire from short range. Two or three such sections of turret fighters, simultaneously engaging a bomber formation from different directions, could thus inflict heavy casualties.

In January 1940 the Aeroplane and Armament Experimental Establishment at Boscombe Down issued a paper entitled *The Tactical Employment of the Turret Fighter with Particular Reference to the Defiant Aircraft*. This stated that although a fighter with fixed guns could almost invariably fly faster than a turret fighter, the latter could play a useful role even if its speed was little greater than that of the enemy bombers it was to engage. The paper went on to outline the advantages that the turret fighter was expected to bring to an engagement:

(a) Its presence, even as a minority amongst the fighters, will force the enemy to arm offensively and even defensively against attacks from all directions and this will cause important sacrifices of speed, range and carrying power. Adequate defensive armour against even .303-in ammunition, fired from all directions, may be prohibitively heavy, so that a turret fighter may be able to use light ammunition [i.e. that from rifle calibre weapons] with a great volume of fire, long after the fixed gun fighters and bombers have been forced to use ammunition of much greater weight and smaller relative fire volume.

(b) Turret fighters working together or in co-operation with fixed gun fighters can attack a bomber or formation of bombers from many directions simultaneously, and this may prove to be a vitally important factor.

(c) Since a [turret] fighter can, within limits, choose the range, fire direction and speed of attack, the turret fighter can make use of the fact that, when travelling on a course parallel with that of the bomber at an excess speed, the sighting allowance [i.e. deflection] for fire from fighter to bomber may be zero or very small while that from the bomber to fighter is necessarily large. This fact can always be used to the advantage of the fighter . . .

In considering the role planned for the turret fighter, RAF tacticians were not talking about engaging single enemy bombers. Conventional fixed-gun fighters were perfectly well able to deal with those. The case for the turret fighter becomes clearer when considering a much larger engagement, for example when two or three sections each of three turret fighters engage a formation of twenty or more bombers.

The *Luftwaffe* bomber types of the early war period, the Dornier Do 17, the Heinkel He 111 and the Junkers Ju 88, all employed hand-held guns mounted on fixed pivots. In the lower hemisphere, these weapons provided only a limited defensive coverage. There was plenty of room to the side and beneath a bomber formation, from which a section of turret fighters could engage while themselves remaining immune from effective return fire.

For the bomber crews there would be the morale-shattering prospect of suffering withering fire from close range, while being unable to hit back at their tormentors. The only way for an engaged bomber or bombers to avoid that torrent of fire would be to break out of formation — and render themselves vulnerable to attack from conventional fighters.

To sum up: those commentators who write off the turret fighter as merely 'a bomber destroyer', while failing to describe its tactical rationale, sell the aircraft short. The turret fighter was much more than 'a bomber destroyer'; it was 'a bomber formation destroyer'.

So much for the theory. We shall see how well these planned tactics would play out, when tested in the harsh school of combat.

seater with its armament of four machine guns mounted in a turret, was designed to engage unescorted bomber formations; it had not been designed to dogfight with enemy single-seaters. Soon after they left the coast near Folkestone the Defiants were 'bounced' by Messerschmitt 109s, again of *Jagdgeschwader* 51. Two British fighters were shot down immediately and during the subsequent dogfight, the inferiority of the turret fighter in this type of action was clearly demonstrated. By attacking from behind and below, the Messerschmitt pilots kept outside the Defiant's return fire, and the two-seaters had neither the speed nor manoeuvrability to avoid these tactics. Twelve Hurricanes from No 111 Squadron were sent to assist the Defiants, but they arrived only in time to save the two-seaters from complete annihilation. Of the nine Defiants only three survived, and one of those suffered damage. Of the eighteen men aboard in the Defiants, ten were killed and two wounded. Only one Messerschmitt was shot down.

For Air Chief Marshal Dowding the lessons of the 19 July action were clear enough. Within two days both Defiant squadrons were on their way to quiet areas in the north where they would be safe from enemy single-seaters.

A further lesson during the early engagements was that the German fighter sweeps were inflicting unacceptably severe losses on the British fighter units they encountered. Now the RAF Sector controllers received orders to vector their fighters only against enemy formations thought to include bombers. Whenever possible, the enemy fighter sweeps were to be left alone. For its part, the *Luftwaffe* learned that unescorted bombers operating by day over the Channel or southern England could expect short shrift if they were intercepted by British fighters.

Inexorably the pace of fighting continued to accelerate. On 8 August there was a fierce air battle around the convoy 'Peewit' in the Channel. Out of twenty ships in the original convoy, four were sunk and six damaged. In the air fighting around the convoy, the *Luftwaffe* lost 28 aircraft and Fighter Command lost 19.

On 11 August the *Luftwaffe* launched its first large-scale attack on a target in Britain. Following a series of feints by fighters in the Dover area, a force of about seventy Heinkel He 111s and Junkers Ju 88s, escorted by nearly one hundred Messerschmitt Bf 109s and Bf 110s, made for the naval base at Portland. Eight squadrons of Spitfires and Hurricanes were scrambled to intercept the raiders, and in the ensuing action the *Luftwaffe* lost 40 aircraft while the RAF lost 26 fighters.

On 12 August there was a similar heavy attack on Portsmouth, with subsidiary attacks by dive-bombers against several targets including the Chain Home radar stations at Pevensey, Rye, Dover, Dunkirk (in Kent) and Ventnor. These radar stations were small pinpoint targets, however. They proved difficult to hit, and even more difficult to put out of action for any length of time. Following hasty repairs, all those radar stations, except one, were back in operation by the following day.

During the 34-day period of the initial skirmishes, between 10 July and 12 August, the *Luftwaffe* lost 261 aircraft and Fighter Command 127. That gave a loss ratio of just over 2:1 in favour of the RAF but that had been during a period of small-scale actions in which each side sounded out its opponent's strengths and weaknesses. The scale of the actions thus far had put neither air force to any real test. On 12 August, *Luftflotten* 2, 3 and 5 received orders to commence a series of all-out damaging attacks aimed at destroying RAF Fighter Command as an effective fighting force. The new phase of the German attack was scheduled to begin on 13 August.

THE INITIAL SKIRMISHES – AIRCRAFT LOSSES

This table lists the aircraft lost or damaged beyond repair in combat missions during each 24-hour period. In the case of the *Luftwaffe*, losses of all types of aircraft engaged in operations against Britain are listed. In the case of the RAF the list gives fighters destroyed in the air or on the ground.

Date	Luftwaffe	RAF	Action
10 July	12	3	Heavy attack on shipping.
11 July	16	6	Heavy attacks on ports and shipping.
12 July	8	3	Attacks on ports and shipping.
13 July	6	2	Attacks on shipping.
14 July	3	1	Attack on shipping.
15 July	3	1	Attack on shipping.
16 July	3	0	Bad weather restricted flying.
17 July	2	1	Poor weather, attack on shipping.
18 July	4	5	Attacks on ports and shipping.
19 July	5	10	Attack on Dover.
20 July	10	8	Attacks on shipping.
21 July	8	2	Attacks on shipping.
22 July	1	1	Attacks on ports and shipping.
23 July	2	0	Attacks on shipping and other targets.
24 July	10	3	Attacks on shipping.
25 July	13	6	Heavy attacks on shipping.
26 July	3	1	Poor weather, little activity.
27 July	4	2	Attacks on shipping.
28 July	10	2	Attacks on ports and shipping.
29 July	12	5	Attacks on shipping.
30 July	6	0	Attacks on shipping.
31 July	3	3	Attacks on shipping.
1 August	7	3	Attacks on shipping.
2 August	4	0	Attacks on shipping.
3 August	4	0	Attacks on shipping.
4 August	0	0	Little activity.
5 August	3	1	Attacks on shipping.
6 August	0	0	Little activity.
7 August	1	0	Attacks on shipping.
8 August	28	19	Large scale attacks on convoy.
9 August	4	0	Little activity.
10 August	0	0	Little activity.
11 August	40	26	Heavy attacks on shipping and Portland.
12 August	26	13	Attacks on shipping and radar stations.
TOTALS	**261**	**127**	

Air Fighting Tactics

At the beginning of the Second World War few air forces had a clear idea of how, or even if, their fighters would engage those of the enemy. In each case the fighters had been designed primarily to engage enemy bombers, and many experts believed that the increases in performance since the First World War had made dogfighting a thing of the past. The Royal Air Force *Manual of Air Tactics*, 1938 edition, solemnly stated:

'Manoeuvre at high speeds in air fighting is not now practicable, because the effect of gravity on the human body during rapid changes of direction at high speed causes a temporary loss of consciousness, deflection shooting becomes difficult and accuracy is hard to obtain.'

As a result RAF fighter tactics were designed to defeat formations of bombers, and the possibility of fighter-versus-fighter combat was almost ignored.

To engage a formation of bombers effectively it was necessary to employ the concentrated fire power of a large number of fighters. Thus the RAF planned to use a squadron formation of twelve aircraft, divided into four sections each of three aircraft. During cruising flight the sections flew in V formation, the commander flew in the middle of the leading V and the other three Vs flew behind in close line astern. The fighters flew close together with about one wingspan, approximately 12 yards, between them. As well as giving concentrated fire power, this type of formation was the best for the penetration of cloud – an important factor to be considered in air operations over northern Europe.

The squadron commander was to lead his formation to a position on the flank of the enemy bomber formation once there he ordered his sections into echelon, and took his own section in to attack. Each fighter pilot was to move into a firing position behind an enemy bomber where (again in the words of the 1938 RAF *Manual of Air Tactics*):

'... he stays until either he has exhausted his ammunition, the target aircraft has been shot down, or he himself has been shot down or his engine put out of action.'

The other sections were to queue up behind that of the leader, and attack in turn after the section in front had broken away. This tactical formation and type of attack was not the only one in use in the RAF, but it was representative of the rigid tactical thinking existing in this air force and several others before the war.

In 1939 the only evidence available to most air forces on the nature of modern air warfare was what could be gleaned from reports from the Spanish Civil War. Studying

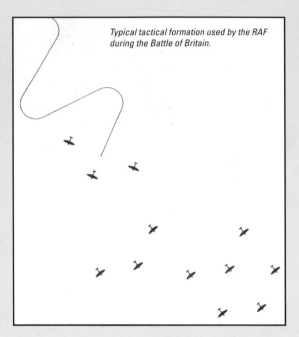

Typical tactical formation used by the RAF during the Battle of Britain.

such reports was like perusing the Bible: no matter what one was trying to prove, one was almost certain to find evidence to support it. The conflict in Spain had shown that bombers almost always got through to their targets, and if conditions were favourable they could cause severe damage. There had been a great deal of scrappy fighter-versus-fighter combat, but most of it was inconclusive and little of it was between fighters of modern design.

Only in Germany were the lessons of the Spanish Civil War put to good use. The *Luftwaffe* emerged from the conflict with no doubt that air combat between modern fighters, although difficult, was likely to occur in any future war. Over Spain the German pilots had experimented with a novel set of tactics for fighters based on the *Rotte*, a widely spaced pair of aircraft. During cruising flight the two aircraft flew about 182 metres (200 yards) apart, almost in line abreast with the leader slightly ahead; each pilot concentrated his search inwards to cover his partner's blind area behind and below. During combat against enemy fighters the wingman kept watch for enemy aircraft attacking from behind, allowing the leader to concentrate his full attention on the enemy aircraft he was going after.

Two *Rotten* made up a *Schwarm* of four aircraft, flying in what became known as a 'finger-four' formation because of its resemblance to the fingers of a hand, with the leading *Rotte* to one side and slightly ahead of the other, and the aircraft were stepped down into the sun. With its component

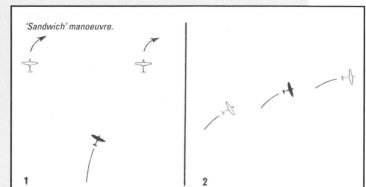

The 'cross-over' turn.

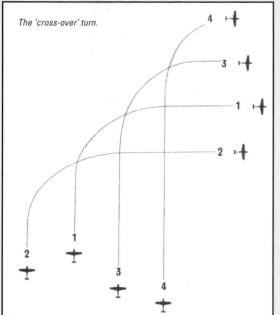

'Sandwich' manoeuvre.

1   2

aircraft spaced about 182 metres (200 yards) apart, the *Schwarm* was approximately 550 metres (600 yards) wide, making it almost impossible for the aircraft to hold position during a tight turn at high speed. The answer was the 'cross-over' turn: each aircraft turned as tightly as it could, and simply swapped sides in the formation.

In determining the effectiveness of a combat formation for fighters, three factors need to be considered: first, the ability of the formation to manoeuvre while maintaining cohesion; secondly, the ability of the pilots to cover each others' blind areas and thus prevent a surprise attack on any of the aircraft; and, thirdly, the ability of each aircraft in the formation to receive near immediate support from the others if it came under attack.

On each of these three criteria, the German tactical

formations were greatly superior to the tight formation used by the RAF. Using the 'cross-over' turn, the *Schwarm* could turn as tightly as individual aircraft were able; in the tight formations used by the RAF, the rate of turn was limited by the need to fly round the aircraft on the inside of the 'V. In cruising flight, every pilot in a Schwarm searched for the enemy, and each man was positioned to see into his comrades' blind areas. In the tight formations used by the RAF, only the leader searched for the enemy while the other pilots concentrated on holding formation. Thus there was poor coverage of the all-important sector behind and below the formation. If an aircraft in a *Rotte* or a *Schwarm* was attacked from behind, a simple turn would result in the attacker being 'sandwiched'; if the rear section of a tight formation came under attack, the action was usually over before others in the formation could come to its aid.

Over France, and during the early part of the Battle of Britain, the RAF's fighters were tactically outclassed by their German counterparts. The middle of a battle is no place for a radical change in tactics, and the RAF had to make the best use it could of the tactics in which its pilots had been trained. The V formation was widened out to allow pilots to spend more time searching for the enemy rather than holding an exact distance from their neighbours; and one section, led by an experienced pilot, flew a weaving course about 1,000 feet above the main formation, keeping watch for the enemy to prevent surprise attack. These two steps greatly improved the search and mutual support capabilities of the fighter formation, although they did little to improve its ability to turn tightly without losing cohesion.

It remained to be seen whether these changes would allow RAF fighters to challenge those of the *Luftwaffe* on equal terms.

Messerschmitt Bf 109 Es of JG 27, flying in an open Schwarm formation.

Supermarine Spitfire

The Supermarine Spitfire, the highest-performance fighter type in the Royal Air Force, equipped nineteen squadrons during the Battle. Carrying the equipment and armour standard on aircraft in the summer of 1940, the Mark I had a maximum speed of 345 mph. The Mark II, which entered service that September, had a more powerful engine and a maximum speed of 354 mph. Standard armament was eight .303-in machine guns, but a few Spitfires took part in the Battle modified to carry two 20 mm cannon – although these cannon-armed versions were unpopular due to stoppages in combat.

Armourers feverishly re-arm a Spitfire between sorties during the battle. The eight-gun Spitfire (and Hurricane) demanded considerable effort, since cleaning the eight guns, loading eight 300-round belts of ammunition, and checking the compressed air, created quite a workload. Experienced ground-crews could do this in as little as ten minutes.

Although not the same Spitfire pictured above, this photograph shows a fully re-armed aircraft with its engine running while a ground crewman makes last checks with the pilot, before jumping down and removing the wheel chocks. Note the difference in underwing roundel sizes on both these Spitfires and the resealed gun ports with canvas patches.

Messerschmitt Bf 109 E

During the late summer of 1940, Bf 109s started appearing over Britain with yellow or white tactical markings applied to the outer flying surfaces and cowlings. This Bf 109 E shows early application of the orders with only the rudder being so applied.

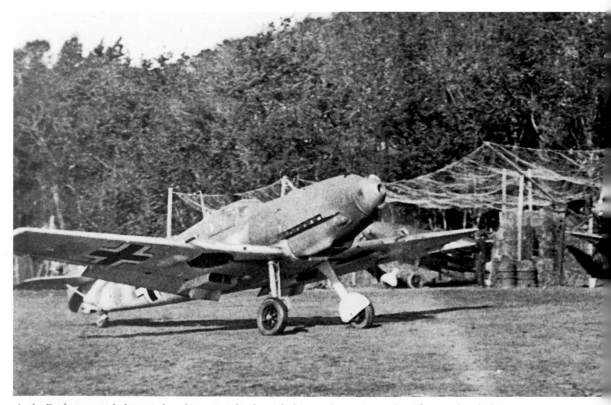

As the Battle progressed, the tactical markings started to be applied in ever larger areas to the airframe – though their appearance differed widely within individual units. These are Bf 109 Es of 1./JG 52 at Calais, probably mid-August 1940 and the aircraft taxiing in the foreground is Oblt. Helmut Bennemann's 'Black 5' which has the entire nose back to the windscreen painted yellow, whereas the aircraft in the background has only its upper cowling in yellow.

The Messerschmitt Bf 109 E was the sole single-engine fighter type operated by the *Luftwaffe* during the Battle of Britain. It had a maximum speed of 570 km/h (354 mph) and a usual armament of two 20 mm cannon and two 7.9 mm machine guns (earlier versions in the battle carried 4 x 7.9 mm machine guns). The type also served as a fighter-bomber in the latter half of the Battle carrying up to 250 kg (550 lbs) of bombs. Though it was initially conceived to fire a cannon through the airscrew spinner, development problems precluded its use until the introduction of the Bf 109 F. The remaining hollow blast tube through the crankcase of the 'E' model was left open. Later in the Battle, the 'E' model was often found with alternate spinner designs with the hole faired over.

The Spitfire Mark I versus the Messerschmitt Bf 109 E

In November 1939 French forces captured an intact example of the Messerschmitt Bf 109 E-3, the latest version of this fighter then in service with the *Luftwaffe*. After testing, the aircraft was handed over to the RAF, and it went to the Royal Aircraft Establishment at Farnborough for a comparative trial against a Spitfire I. The two aircraft were flown in turn by Wing Commander George Stainforth, of Schneider Trophy fame, and the future fighter ace Flight Lieutenant Robert Stanford-Tuck.

The Spitfire employed in the trials had been fitted with the Rotol constant speed propeller. At that time Fighter Command was just commencing a crash programme to fit all Spitfires and Hurricanes with this or the de Havilland constant speed propeller, in place of the previous two-speed type. The constant speed propeller automatically adjusted the pitch angle of the blades, to give the most efficient setting for the airspeed and engine revolutions selected. It also improved the take-off and climbing performance of RAF fighters.

Following the series of comparative flight trials, the Air Tactics Branch of the Air Ministry issued the following report in July 1940:

Comparative Trial between Me 109 and 'Rotol' propeller-equipped Spitfire

1. *The trial commenced with the two aircraft taking off together, with the Spitfire slightly behind and using +6 ¼ lb boost and 3,000 rpm.*
2. *When fully airborne, the pilot of the Spitfire reduced his engine revolutions to 2,650 rpm and was then able to overtake and outclimb the Me 109. At 4,000 feet, the Spitfire pilot was 1,000 feet above the Me 109, from which position he was able to get on to its tail, and remain there within effective range despite all efforts of the pilot of the Me 109 to shake him off.*
3. *The Spitfire then allowed the Me 109 to get on to his tail and attempted to shake him off. This he found quite easy owing to the superior manoeuvrability of his aircraft, particularly in the looping plane and at low speeds between 100 and 140 mph. By executing a steep turn just above stalling speed, he ultimately got back into a position on the tail of the Me 109.*
4. *Another effective form of evasion with the Spitfire was found to be a steep, climbing spiral at 120 mph, using +6 lb boost and 2,650 rpm; in this manoeuvre, the Spitfire gained rapidly on the Me 109, eventually allowing the pilot to execute a half roll, on to the tail of his opponent.*
5. *Comparative speed trials were then carried out, and the Spitfire proved to be considerably the faster of the two, both in acceleration and straight and level flight, without having to make use of the emergency +12 lb boost. During diving trials, the Spitfire pilot found that by engaging fully coarse pitch and using -2 lb boost, his aircraft was superior to the Me 109.*

The Farnborough trial proved to the satisfaction of everyone there that the Spitfire I was greatly superior to the Messerschmitt 109 E – at altitudes around 4,000 feet. The trouble was, however, that German fighter pilots had no intention of conducting low-speed and low-altitude dogfights with enemy fighters in the way the Farnborough trial had suggested. The engine cooling difficulties experienced with the captured Messerschmitt had concealed the fact that when fully serviceable, this aircraft could outclimb the Spitfire at most altitudes. The German pilots' best tactics were therefore to climb above their foe, move into a favourable position for attack, and then deliver a high-speed diving attack before zooming back to safety. If appropriate, and if they had sufficient ammunition, they then repeated the process.

National pride being what it is, the reader will probably not be surprised to learn that a similar trial carried out in Germany produced exactly the opposite result! At the *Luftwaffe* test centre at Rechlin, tests with a captured Spitfire I proved to the satisfaction of everyone there that the Bf 109 was the superior fighter. The Spitfire used in the trials was probably one of those forced down and captured intact at the time of the Dunkirk evacuation in May or June 1940. Like almost all Spitfires in front line service at that time, it was fitted with a two-speed propeller; as a result, its climbing performance was somewhat inferior to that of the Spitfire used in the Farnborough trials. Also, German pilots were quick to grasp the fact that the float carburettor of the Merlin engine fitted to the Spitfire ceased delivering fuel if the pilot pushed down the nose of his aircraft and applied negative 'G', with the result that the engine cut out. The Bf 109 and the Bf 110 were fitted with fuel injector pumps and so did not suffer from this failing.

One famous German pilot who tried his hand with both the Spitfire and the Hurricane during the early summer of 1940 was *Hauptmann* Werner Moelders; with 25 aerial victories, the then top-scoring *Luftwaffe* fighter pilot. He afterwards wrote: *'It was very interesting to carry out the flight trials at Rechlin with the Spitfire and the Hurricane. Both types are very simple to fly compared with our aircraft, and childishly easy to take-off and land. The Hurricane is very good-natured and turns well, but its performance is decidedly inferior to that of the Bf 109. It has strong stick forces and is "lazy" on the ailerons.*

'The Spitfire is one class better. It handles well, is light on the controls, faultless in the turn and has a performance approaching that of the Bf 109. As a fighting aircraft, however, it is miserable. A sudden push forward on the stick will cause the motor to cut; and because the propeller has only two pitch settings [take-off and cruise], in a rapidly changing air combat situation the motor is either overspending or else is not being used to the full.'

The two nations' trials produced results that were valid only up to a point. The British trial had been flown at medium altitude to simulate a low-speed turning fight, because there the Spitfire was better. The German trial had been flown at higher altitude simulating a high-speed combat, because there the Bf 109 was better. During the Battle of Britain most fighter-versus-fighter combats took place at altitudes between 13,000 and 20,000 feet, because that was where the German bombers were. And in that height band the performances of the Spitfire I and the Messerschmitt 109 E were rather more equal than either nations' flight trials had suggested. In the fleeting combats that came to be normal between fighters, tactical initiative counted for a great deal more than the relatively minor advantages and disadvantages of the two main fighter types.

Messerschmitt Bf 109 E-1, the earliest version of the 'E' to see combat with the RAF during the Battle of France and later the Battle of Britain. It was used right through the Battle alongside the E-3 and E-4 – it primarily differed from the later variants in having no wing cannon fitted, these being 7.9 mm machine guns with another two in the upper cowling.

Oberleutnant Julius Neumann of Jagdgeschwader 27.

A New Opponent for the Luftwaffe

A *Luftwaffe* pilot gives his impressions of his first encounters with the Royal Air Force:

'During the campaign in France it was difficult to compare our Messerschmitt 109 with the French Morane or Curtiss fighters, because I never had a dogfight with either of them. I saw only one Morane during the entire campaign, and it was disappearing in the distance.

'Our Geschwader had very little dogfighting experience until the Dunkirk action, where it met the Royal Air Force for the first time in numbers. Our pilots came back with the highest respect for the enemy. I personally did not experience dogfighting until early in August, when I became embroiled with British fighters over the Isle of Wight. And we felt we were dealing with a pilot-aircraft combination as good as our own. The longer serving RAF pilots had considerable flying experience, they were well trained and they knew what they were fighting for. Of course there were young and inexperienced pilots too, but we had the feeling that there was a backbone of very well trained and experienced pilots.'

Oberleutnant Julius Neumann, Messerschmitt Bf 109 pilot of *Jagdgeschwader* 27

The Arrival of a New Pilot

A new pilot describes his arrival at No 111 Squadron at Croydon, having completed his flying training:

'When I arrived at Croydon after training the CO asked me how many [flying] hours I had on the Hurricane. I said I had fifteen. He said 'That's no good to me. You will fly three hours each morning and two each afternoon until you have 45 hours on type.'

'When I had 45 hours on the Hurricane I was called in front of the CO for a ten-minute lecture on how to fight the Hun. It was all high falutin' stuff, delivered while I stood in front of him to attention with my hat on. He said things like "The Hun is a very tricky chap, Newton. You've got be very wary." The only thing I got out of the interview was that when I was flying alone and the enemy was around, I was not to fly straight for more than two seconds. At the end of the chat the CO said: "You've done 45 hours flying on the Hurricane, as from tomorrow you will be Blue 3." Gradually I gained experience in formation flying and operational scrambles etc. My biggest worry was falling away from the fight and being called a coward.'

Sergeant Harry Newton, Hurricane pilot, No 111 Squadron

Supermarine Spitfire Mk I, QV-K, P9386, flown by Squadron Leader Brian Lane, CO of 19 Squadron, Duxford, in September 1940. Brian Lane was credited with four aerial victories during the Battle, plus one before and one after, to take his total score to six. He was killed in action in December 1942.

A Hawker Hurricane Mk 1, N2359, YB-J, of No 17 Squadron based at Debden in September 1940.

The Reluctant Warrior

'When the war broke out all of the pilots of No 17 Squadron had been together for at least three years. Obviously we knew each other very well. When we began to lose such people it really hit me. Newcomers joined the squadron, but one never got to know them as well as our pre-war comrades.

'I didn't really like the idea of shooting down people, or trying to. But it was a question of them or us. I had joined the RAF and trained as a fighter pilot. When the war came along I thought "This is it, I've got to earn my money now." I knew what I had to do, and I did the best I could. Some of the youngsters on the squadron would really upset me when they glorified in the killing. I couldn't adopt that sort of attitude.'

Sergeant John Etherington, Hurricane pilot, No 17 Squadron

Scenes at the German fighter airfield at Caffiers near Calais, home of 3./JG 26 during the Battle of Britain, showing the unit's Bf 109s in their sandbagged and camouflaged revetments.

Another view of Bf 109s of 3./JG 26 at Caffiers near Calais.

A Heinkel He 115 floatplane of Küstenfliegergruppe 506. During the Battle this unit was based in Norway and northern Germany, from where it conducted night minelaying operations off ports in Great Britain.

Above and right: The Heinkel He 59 floatplane, an obsolete torpedo-bomber, served in the air-sea rescue role during the Battle.

A Focke-Wulf Fw 200 Condor of Kampfgeschwader 40. This unit flew anti-shipping missions over the Atlantic to the west of the British Isles, plying between bases at Bordeaux in France and Trondheim in Norway during the Battle. This Fw 200 C-2, W.Nr. 0023, F8+EH, is believed to have been flown at one time by the Staffelkapitan of 1./KG 40.

Bomber crewmen of Kampfgeschwader 76 trying out one of the rubber dinghies issued to the unit, as part of the preparation for over-water missions against Britain.

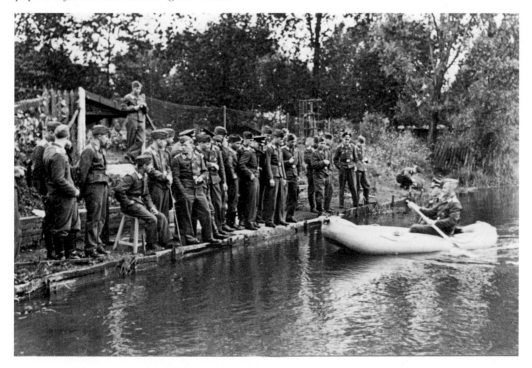

Men of the Luftwaffe

Adolf Galland was born on 19 March 1912 in Westerholt, Westphalia. The son of an estate manager, he spent his childhood in a middle-class rural home in an environment of strict religious discipline. He enjoyed sports and music rather than academic study and at an early age developed a fondness for building wooden model aeroplanes. Qualifying as a glider pilot in 1931, he joined the fledgling Luftwaffe in 1933 and took part in a rudimentary and semi-clandestine training course for future German military airmen in Italy. In April 1937, he volunteered for more clandestine service, this time with the Legion Condor in Spain and flew as Staffelkapitän of 3./J 88 flying He 51s, not so much as the fighter pilot he wanted to be, but rather as a ground-attack flier in which role he became instrumental in the development of close-support tactics. The regular reports that he despatched to his superiors were well received.

On his return from Spain in August 1938, the raven-haired, cigar-smoking young officer spent time working for the RLM where he was involved in the establishment of the early Schlachtgruppen, before flying 87 ground-support missions in Poland in a Hs 123 as a Staffelkapitän with II.(Sch)/LG 2. In February 1940, he was finally posted to a fighter role with Stab/JG 27 at Krefeld. Three months later, German forces attacked in the West.

Although Galland found himself in a semi-administrative role drawing up pilot rosters, arranging unit-level meetings and liaising with Fliegerkorps VIII, JG 27's immediate command organisation, he was still able to account for 12 enemy aircraft shot down by 9 June, including two Spitfires. By this time, Galland had been transferred again, this time as Gruppenkommandeur with III./JG 26 at Capelle in France and he led this unit with distinction during the battles against the RAF over the English Channel that summer. In late August, Göring had decided to replace a number of those he deemed to be his older and more 'staid' unit commanders with younger, more innovative officers. It is perhaps not surprising that the exploits and accomplishments of the dashing, extrovert Galland with his passion for hunting and shooting, attracted Göring since he embodied all that was required of the modern fighter pilot.

On 22 August, three weeks after he had been awarded the Knight's Cross with 17 victories to his credit, the newly promoted Major Galland was propelled to the position of Kommodore of JG 26, replacing Major Gotthardt Handrick, an officer whom Göring apparently disliked. Nevertheless, for his part, Galland had never been afraid to express his fears and misgivings to those in high command. During the Battle of Britain, he took great pains to spell out to Göring the folly of trying to take on the Spitfire in turning dog-fights in which he knew the RAF fighter enjoyed superior performance. Instead, Galland pushed for hit-and-run tactics which advantaged the fast Bf 109.

In November 1941, Galland, by now one of the few holders of the coveted Knight's Cross with Oakleaves and Swords (and the first recipient of the Swords), was plucked from his command of JG 26 to replace his 'old rival' Werner Mölders as General der Jagdflieger, following Mölders death in an air crash.

Werner Mölders was a leading German fighter ace in the Spanish Civil War. Mölders became the first pilot in aviation history to claim 100 aerial victories – that is, 100 aerial combat encounters resulting in the destruction of the enemy aircraft, and was highly decorated for his achievements. He was instrumental in the development of new fighter tactics which led to the 'finger-four' formation (see pages. 16-17). He died in the crash of an He 111, whilst on his way to attend the funeral of Ernst Udet.

Major Helmut Wick, holder of the Knight's Cross of the Iron Cross with Oakleaves. He scored all of his 56 kills against the Western Allies flying the Messerschmitt Bf 109 E. He was shot down and killed off the Isle of Wight on 28 November 1940, by F/Lt John Dundas who was himself shot down and killed immediately afterwards by Wick's wingman.

Bf 109 pilots of III./JG 26. From left to right: Leutnant Lüdewig, Leutnant Heinz Ebeling, Oberleutnant Gerhard Schöpfel, Oberleutnant Josef Haiböck and Leutnant Hans Nauman.

Right: Hauptmann Karl Ebbinghausen, commander of II./JG 26, pictured in his Bf 109. Ebbinghausen was killed in action on 16 August.

Major Helmut Bode, Junkers Ju 87 pilot and Kommandeur of III./St.G 77

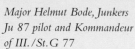

Major Victor von Lossberg, Heinkel He 111 pilot and Kommandeur of III./KG 26.

Leutnant Wilhelm Herget, Bf 110 pilot of II./ZG 76.

Leutnant Rudolf Ahrens, a Heinkel He 111 pilot of Kampfgeschwader 1, was shot down and captured on 18 August.

Some of 'The Few'

Above and right: Squadron Leader Douglas Bader, the famous pilot who had both of his legs amputated following a flying accident before the war. He flew Hurricanes and commanded No 242 Squadron. He also led the Duxford 'Big Wing' during the Battle.

Squadron Leader Robert Stanford Tuck flew Spitfires with No 92 Squadron early in the battle and later commanded No 257 Squadron with Hurricanes.

Spitfire pilots from No 19 Squadron illustrate the varied origins of those who flew with RAF Fighter Command in September 1940. From left to right Pilot Officer 'Jock' Cunningham from Glasgow; Lieutenant 'The Admiral' Blake, one of several Fleet Air Arm fighter pilots loaned to Fighter Command; Flight Lieutenant F. Dolezahl, a Czech who escaped from his country to join the French Air Force, then escaped again to join the RAF; and Flying Officer F. Brinsden, a New Zealander. Lieutenant Blake was killed in action on 29 October.

Left: Sergeant Herbert Hallowes, a Hurricane pilot of No 43 Squadron.

Flying Officer John Hardacre, a Hurricane pilot with No 504 Squadron. He was killed in action on 30 September.

Above: Flight Sergeant Phil Tew, a Spitfire pilot with No 54 Squadron.

Flying Officer Stefan Witorzenc, from Poland, flew Hurricanes with No 501 Squadron.

Right: Flying Officer 'Uncle Sam' Leckrone, an American volunteer, fought during the Battle with Nos 616 and 19 Squadrons flying Spitfires. He later would become a founder member of No 71, the first U.S. 'Eagle' Squadron.

Ground Crews

During the Battle, both sides depended on the ability of their ground crews to carry out rapid turn-around, refuelling, re-arming and to clear minor faults, so pilots and aircrew could return to the fray quickly. Here, Spitfires of No 66 Squadron are refuelled from a Crossley tanker, probably at Biggin Hill.

Armourers reloading the guns on a Hurricane between sorties, with the pilot waiting patiently in his cockpit.

The Ground Crews

'The ground crews were past all praise. If we had long hours, they had longer ones by far. They were always laughing and ragging round the place and betting cigarettes or drinks as to whether A Flight would do better than B Flight or whether such and such a pilot would get one or two today.

'How Tubby, the Squadron Engineer Officer, continued to render at least fifteen out of about twenty Hurricanes serviceable at every readiness period is a secret that will die with him. A lot of publicity and glamour comes the way of the fighter pilot, but not all the praise in the world would do justice to these "back room boys".'

Squadron Leader Michael Crossley, Commanding No 32 Squadron with Hurricanes

'Each Staffel had its own dispersal area around the perimeter of the airfield at Antwerp. When we arrived the Dornier's engines had been warmed up and my mechanic, Gefreiter Erich Treder, said "Maschine klar!" I did not do a walk-round check of the aircraft. If Treder said an aircraft was cleared for flight that was as good as a gold-stamped guarantee.'

Feldwebel Horst Schultz, Dornier Do 17 pilot, *Kampfgeschwader* 3

In many cases during the Battle, Luftwaffe flying units had to operate from hastily-prepared airfields, with most of the servicing work carried out in the open. This Bf 109 of III./JG 26 is receiving an engine change at Caffiers.

A Messerschmitt Bf 110 of ZG 76 undergoes an engine change at Laval.

Silent sentinels. The Chain Home radar station at Swingate near Dover, showing the 350-foot high towers carrying the transmitter aerials, and the 240-foot high wooden towers carrying the receiver aerials. Although these towers might appear fragile, the openwork structures presented a small area to blast or fragmentation effects and they proved difficult to knock down.

An Observer Corps look-out post. Manned by civilian volunteers, a web of these posts tracked enemy formations once they had crossed the English coast and were heading inland.

A Bofors 40 mm light anti-aircraft gun. This weapon fired 2-lb shells at a rate of 120 shells per minute, and was lethally effective against low-flying aircraft. However, far too few Bofors guns were available to defend airfields and other vital points during the summer of 1940.

Left: A four-gun battery belonging to the 52nd Heavy Anti-Aircraft Regiment, in position near Barking, Essex. The 4.5-in gun was the latest and heaviest anti-aircraft weapon used by the Royal Artillery during the Battle, and it fired 55-lb shells at a rate of eight per minute.

Above: Shooting down barrage balloons became a popular pastime for Messerschmitt pilots with time on their hands. Here balloons are seen going down on fire over Gosport.

Left: A barrage balloon flying from the grassed area to the south of the Houses of Parliament at Westminster in London. These ungainly hydrogen-filled gasbags were 62 feet long and 25 feet in diameter, and had a maximum effective flying altitude of about 5,000 feet. They were dotted randomly over targets to be defended and were intended as a deterrent against low-flying aircraft and dive-bombers attempting to press home their accurate attacks to low altitude.

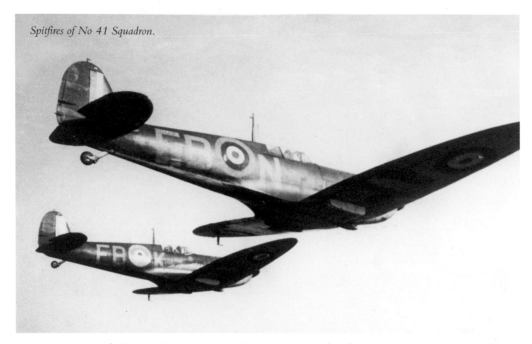

Spitfires of No 41 Squadron.

An armourer at Duxford re-arms the .303-inch machine guns on a Spitfire of No 19 Squadron during the battle.

THE ASSAULT ON THE AIRFIELDS CHAPTER 2

'You can squeeze a bee in your hand until it suffocates.

But it will not suffocate without having stung you.'

JEAN PAULAN

THE actions in July and the early part of August were only a prelude to the main thrust by the *Luftwaffe*, and it was on 13 August that the Battle, in German eyes, really began. On that day the *Luftwaffe* launched a total of 1,485 sorties against the British Isles, hitting naval targets at Portland and Southampton and the airfields at Detling and Eastchurch. During the day's battles the *Luftwaffe* lost thirty-nine aircraft and the RAF lost fourteen.

On the next day, the 14th, the *Luftwaffe* mounted attacks on airfields, although with rather less aircraft. On the 15th the Germans returned in force, with large-scale attacks on airfields and radar stations. From its bases in Norway and Denmark, Luftflotte 5 sent formations of He 111s escorted by Bf 110s, and unescorted Ju 88s, to attack targets in northern England. The intention was to catch Fighter Command off balance with attacks from an unexpected direction. Thanks to the advanced warning provided by radar, however, the raiders failed utterly – the attacking forces were all intercepted and suffered heavy losses as a result. In the course of the various actions that day the *Luftwaffe* lost 79 aircraft while the RAF lost 34. Thereafter *Luftflotte* 5 played little further part in the Battle, and several of its bomber units were transferred to *Luftflotten* 2 and 3 based in France, Holland and Belgium.

Thus began the series of large-scale hard-fought actions that was to continue with few breaks over the next six weeks. Each of the actions contained features unique to itself and it would be misleading to describe any of them as 'typical'. Nevertheless the series of engagements on Sunday, 18 August fit well into the broad pattern of those of the initial phase of the Battle, and will serve to illustrate the variety in the methods of attack employed by the *Luftwaffe* bomber force as well as the defensive tactics used by Fighter Command. This day's events shall, therefore, be examined in detail.

For 18 August, the *Luftwaffe* had planned an ambitious programme of attacks aimed at the four most important British fighter airfields in south-eastern England: Biggin Hill, Kenley, Hornchurch and North Weald. These airfields lay further inland than any previously attacked on a considerable scale. In addition, a large force of Stukas was to attack airfields and a radar station in the Portsmouth area. Thus the stage was set for the action that would see the destruction of more aircraft than any other during the Battle of Britain – 'The Hardest Day'.

It was a beautiful summer's day, with blue skies and just a few wisps of cloud. The morning began quietly enough, with single German reconnaissance aircraft making fleeting high-altitude incursions over southern England to photograph potential targets and report on the weather. From time to time British fighters were scrambled to intercept these intruders, but the latter proved difficult targets and only one was shot down.

The first large-scale attack opened shortly after noon, when the radar stations in south-eastern England began reporting concentrations of enemy aircraft assembling over the Pas de Calais area. In the vanguard of the raiding force were thirty-nine Do 17s and Ju 88s of

Continued on page 44

The author standing outside the entrance to No 11 Group's underground operations room at Uxbridge. The operations room has been preserved in its 1940 condition, and it is open to visitors by prior arrangement.

Below and opposite page: Inside the operations room at Uxbridge, showing the situation map and the fighter controllers' gallery.

In the No 11 Group Plotting Room at Uxbridge

'The whole thing could best be described as "organised chaos". When things got going, plots from the filter room were coming through at about five per minute on each track. The room pictured the scene of battle with raids on the table, and the squadron boards showing the information given by our controller whose voice boomed out continually. Girls would be calling for new counters to update their blocks, runners would be dashing to get them from the table beside the plotting map. If one asked for one thing and one's neighbour asked for something else, it was a matter of who shouted loudest! It was all so unlike the quiet, relaxed atmosphere often depicted in films. Looking down on us from behind the soundproof glass were the duty fighter controller and his assistants. They seemed so calm, so removed from the hubbub below. If things there had been as chaotic as they were with us, I don't think we could have won the battle.'

Aircraftwoman Vera Saies, aircraft plotter, No 11 Group Operations Room, Uxbridge.

Heinkel He 111

The Heinkel He 111 was the main twin-engine bomber type used by the *Luftwaffe* during the Battle. Normally it carried a crew of four: pilot, navigator/bomb-aimer/front gunner, radio operator/rear gunner and flight engineer/ventral gunner. Sometimes a fifth man was carried to operate the guns firing from each side of the fuselage. Cruising speed in formation was 306 km/h (190 mph), maximum speed was (415 km/h) 258 mph. It carried an armament of up to six 7.9 mm machine-guns in separate mountings, and a bomb load of up to 1,500 kg (3,300 lbs).

Underside view of a He 111 showing the uniqe stowage of the bombs, in vertical racks prior to being release.

KENLEY - A TYPICAL RAF FIGHTER AIRFIELD

RAF Kenley lay thirteen miles south of the centre of London. During the initial stages of the Battle of Britain, the airfield was the home of No 64 Squadron with Spitfires and No 615 Squadron with Hurricanes. The fighter station had a complement of 30 officers, 600 airmen and about 100 airwomen. In addition, to protect the base from air or surface attack, there were about 100 soldiers – anti-aircraft gunners and infantrymen. The airfield was protected by four 40 mm Bofors guns, two obsolete 3-in anti-aircraft guns and a few .303-in Lewis guns and 20 mm Hispano cannon on ground mountings.

Until 1939, Kenley had been a grass airfield. But in order to permit all-weather operations, two 800-yard concrete runways had been laid out. The fighters operated from the runways or the grass as convenient. A perimeter track, nearly a mile-and-a half long, surrounded the landing ground, and jutting off from it at intervals ran twelve lead-offs to the protective revetments for the fighters. Each revetment was surrounded on three sides by an 8-foot-high earth-and-brick blast wall, which from above resembled a letter `E', to accommodate two fighters in each. The airfield had sufficient revetments to provide for 24 fighters. Any remaining aircraft were dispersed around the open ground. On the south side of the airfield were four hangars and the station's engineering and administrative buildings. On the eastern edge was the Sector Operations Room whose controllers directed into action the fighters based at Kenley and the nearby airfield at Croydon.

Kampfgeschwader 76, flying at 3650 metres (12,000 feet) and bound for the airfield at Kenley. Also, as yet unseen on the British radar, were nine more Dorniers of the 9. *Staffel* of *Kampfgeschwader* 76 flying just above the waves; these aircraft were to deliver a surprise attack on Kenley from low altitude. About 24 kilometres (15 miles) behind the leading high-altitude raiding force came a second large force comprising sixty He 111s of *Kampfgeschwader* 1, making for Biggin Hill airfield. Escorting the high flying bombers were more than a hundred and fifty Bf 109 and Bf 110 fighters.

From their underground operations room at Uxbridge, the controllers of No 11 Group of Fighter Command disposed their squadrons to contest the enemy incursion. One squadron with twelve Hurricanes, No 501, was already in the process of moving to another airfield. It now received orders to climb into position to meet the enemy. Within minutes, eight further squadrons had been scrambled and were moving into blocking positions ahead of the raiders.

By 1300 hrs the fighters assigned to intercept the raiders were all airborne and clawing for altitude as they moved into position. Five squadrons with fifty-three Spitfires and Hurricanes moved to patrol the line Canterbury-Margate, to block any possible attack aimed at the port installations along the Thames Estuary or the fighter airfields to the north of it. At the same time four more squadrons, with fifty Spitfires and Hurricanes, were spiralled into position to cover the airfields at Kenley and Biggin Hill.

The first clash took place over Canterbury, and the defenders got the worst of it. *Oberleutnant* Gerhard Schöpfel was leading a *Staffel* of Bf 109s of *Jagdgeschwader* 26 on a free-hunting patrol over Kent when he came upon the Hurricanes of No 501 Squadron in the climb. Ordering the other German fighters to remain at altitude and provide cover only if he requested it, Schöpfel went down to engage the enemy force alone. It was the kind of situation where a single aircraft might sneak into a firing position unseen, while the approach of a larger force of fighters would almost certainly be spotted. The German pilot moved into a position up-sun of his quarry, then eased his Messerschmitt into position close on his intended victim in the Hurricanes' blind zone behind and below. With two short but accurate bursts, Schöpfel despatched the two 'weavers' covering the rear of the formation. Then he closed in behind the remaining Hurricanes, and shot down two more. And still he remained unseen. He might have brought down other Hurricanes had not pieces of debris from his last victim smashed into his propeller and spattered oil over his canopy. As Schöpfel made his escape, his comrades dived to give him cover and an inconclusive dogfight developed.

All in all, Gerhard Schöpfel had fought a brilliant engagement, and one that illustrated that although the RAF had improved its tactics it still had some way to go.

By luck rather than calculated design, both formations of high-altitude bombers passed just out of sight from the main British fighter concentration in the Canterbury-Margate area. The bomber crews saw nothing of the defending fighters until they reached Sevenoaks, when

An Intelligence trap awaiting the *Luftwaffe*

On 17 August the *Luftwaffe* Intelligence issued its latest secret assessment of the current strength of RAF Fighter Command:

'During the period from 1 July to 15 August 1940 the following enemy aircraft were confirmed destroyed by fighter action, Flak and on the ground:

Spitfires	373
Hurricanes	180
Curtis's	9
Defiants	12

'To this figure of 574 enemy fighters destroyed must be added at least 196 lost due to machines involved in crash-landings, landings damaged beyond repair, accidents, etc, giving a total loss of some 770 enemy fighters.

'During the same period, some 270 to 300 new fighters were built, so the net reduction in enemy fighter strength is estimated at about 470. On 1 July the fighter units had 900 modern fighters. So by 16 August there were 430 left; allowing 70 per cent serviceability, there are now 300 combat-ready fighters.

'Unconfirmed but previously reliable reports distribute these combat-ready fighters at present as follows:

South and south-eastern England (south of the line The Wash-Bristol Channel)	200
The Midlands	70
Northern England and Scotland	30'

Author's comment

The 'Curtis's' mentioned in the German report were American-built Curtiss Hawk 75A fighters, a type used in large numbers by the French Air Force. This aircraft was frequently mentioned in German combat reports during the Battle of Britain, but in fact none was operational in the RAF in 1940.

Oberst Schmid had calculated the strength of RAF Fighter Command in mid-August by the simple expedient of adding the 900 fighters he thought it possessed on 1 July, to the 300 new fighters believed to have been delivered by the makers since then. He then subtracted the 770 fighters claimed destroyed in action, to arrive at the figure of 430 aircraft remaining.

It was a simplistic approach to a difficult problem, and in this case it produced a result wildly removed from the truth. In fact, on 1 July, RAF Fighter Command had been somewhat weaker than Schmid estimated: its squadrons then had 786 modern single-engined fighters on strength, 114 less than the German estimate. But Schmid's calculations grossly underestimated the output from Britain's aircraft factories: during July and the first half of August they had turned out about 720 fighters, more than twice the *Luftwaffe* estimate. Moreover, during the same period, instead of the 770 aircraft claimed destroyed by all causes, RAF Fighter Command had, in fact, lost 318 Spitfires, Hurricanes and Defiants - less than half the *Luftwaffe* claim. Caught between the hammer of overestimated losses, and the anvil of underestimated production, Schmid's calculation of 430 fighters remaining was well wide of the mark. By mid-August, Fighter Command's squadrons possessed more than a thousand Spitfires, Hurricanes and Defiants. Of these about 850 were serviceable. In addition, a further 300 fighters were parked in maintenance units, ready for immediate issue to front line units to replace losses.

Thus, in mid-August, RAF Fighter Command's day fighter force was about three times stronger than *Oberst* Schmid had calculated. Inexorably, the process of defeating Fighter Command continued, on paper at least. By the first week in September, Schmid assessed that the force was down to its last few fighters and on the point of collapse. If *Luftwaffe* senior commanders acted on these conclusions, they were about to get the shock of their lives . . .

A Dornier 17 of 9. Staffel, Kampfgeschwader 76. At the base of the nose is the 20 mm MG/FF cannon, carried for strafing ground targets.

Dornier Do 17 Z

Left: Although the unit's main equipme was the He 111, a small number of D Zs were also delivered to KGr 100. Th aircraft, 6N+JT, may have been flown Ergänzungskette which was formed on 24 August 1940.

The port engine of this Do 17 Z of the Geschwader Stab of KG 3 is being run up during a maintenance check.

Above: Major Gabelmann, Kommandeur of IV.(Erg)/KG 3, and his crew stand in front of the camera after completing a successful mission. During the Battle, Gabelmann had commanded I./KG 3, but later became the first leader of the Ergänzungsgruppe when it was established at Chievres in Belgium in either October 1940 or May 1941.

The Dornier Do 17, sometimes referred to as the *Fliegender Bleistift* ('Flying pencil'), was designed as a *Schnellbomber* ('fast bomber'), or light bomber which, in theory, would be so fast that it could out-run defending fighter aircraft. It was used alongside the He 111 and Ju 88 during the Battle of Britain. The type was popular among its crews due to its manoeuvrability at low altitude, which made the Dornier capable of surprise bombing attacks (hence its use on the Kenley raid). Its sleek and thin airframe made it harder to hit than other German bombers, as it presented less of a target area. It carried a crew of four: pilot, bomb aimer/gunner and two gunners. Maximum speed was 426 km/h (265 mph), and it carried 6 x 7.9 MG machine guns, although sometimes the lower machine gun in the glazed nose was replaced by a 20 mm MG FF or MG 151 cannon. Maximum bomb load was 1000 kg (2,205 lbs).

This photograph, taken on the afternoon of 16 August from a Dornier 17 of Kampfgeschwader 76, shows ten Hurricanes climbing into position before delivering their attack. Almost certainly the fighters belonged to No 111 Squadron, which delivered a head-on attack on the bomber's formation soon afterwards. One Hurricane collided with a Dornier and both aircraft crashed near Marden; there were no survivors.

they ran into the four squadrons positioned to defend Biggin Hill and Kenley. It was then that the action began in earnest. The commander of No 32 Squadron, Squadron Leader Mike Crossley, had sighted the incoming enemy bomber formation when it was still several miles away. Now he led his Hurricanes into position for a head-on interception.

Raimund Schultz, a *Luftwaffe* war correspondent aboard one of the Dorniers, afterwards wrote of the subsequent attack: 'Here comes the first fighter, from the left and ahead. Very suddenly he is before our eyes, like a wasp, dashing through our formation. I see the reddish tracer rounds flying back and forth. Everything happens very quickly.'

In one of the Hurricanes, Pilot Officer Alan Eckford loosed off a short burst at one of the Dorniers but then had to push hard on his stick to avoid colliding with it. Once past his victim he looked back and saw the bomber pull up in a drunken half roll, then spin away to earth. Lying on his stomach on the floor of the Dornier and manning the rearwards-firing machine gun, *Oberfeldwebel* Wilhelm Lautersack had heard a crash as Eckford's rounds slammed into the bomber. Then the aircraft began to spin and he was pinned to the floor by the vicious 'G' forces. Lautersack glanced forwards, to see his pilot slumped lifeless against his harness. With a strength born of fear, the German crewman inched his way to the escape hatch in the floor of the cabin, released it and tumbled out. After a long delay he pulled his ripcord and was relieved when the canopy opened with a loud jolt.

Meanwhile Donald MacDonell at the head of No 64 Squadron was leading his Spitfires down to engage the same German formation. 'I gave a quick call "*Freema Squadron, Bandits below! Tally Ho!*" Then down we went in a wide spiral, keeping a wary eye open for the inevitable German fighters.' MacDonell pulled in behind one of the Bf 110 escorts, raked it with his fire, and saw it enter a steep dive with both engines smoking strongly. Shortly afterwards the Spitfires of No 610 Squadron and Hurricanes of No 615 Squadron also joined in the action.

While this was happening, the nine Dorniers of the low-flying attack force had crossed the coast near Beachy Head and were closing on Kenley from the south. The bombers passed over the small market town of Burgess Hill, where people in the streets stood as if glued to the spot gazing up at the low flying bombers. 'At first they did not take us for the enemy, not expecting German aircraft to be flying so low. Then the large crosses on our wings taught them otherwise and in the next instant they were scurrying for cover,' remembered *Unteroffizier* Günther Unger piloting one of the Dorniers.

The hedge-hopping Dorniers of 9. *Staffel* reached Kenley without interference from the defences, but also without the benefit of surprise: the web of Observer Corps posts had

Hauptmann Joachim Roth (right), the commander of 9./KG 76, was navigator aboard the lead aircraft for the low-altitude attack on Kenley on 18 August. Oberleutnant Rudolf Lamberty (right) piloted the lead aircraft.

Below: Photographed from another Do 17 on the Kenley raid, Dorniers of 9.KG 76 are seen approaching Beachy Head at very low altitude.

Unteroffizier Günther Unger.

Above: Günther Unger's Do 17 pictured soon after crossing the coast on 18 August. The town in the background is Seaford. The bomber's shadow indicates that the aircraft was flying at about 18 metres (60 feet) above the ground.

The northern edge of Kenley airfield, pictured during the attack, with cannon shells exploding around a gun position on the ground. The Spitfire in the revetment belonged to No 64 Squadron, and suffered damage during the action.

reported each stage of their progress over Sussex and Surrey. Now, as the bombers ran in to attack Kenley, the airfield's defences were manned and ready.

As the raiders pulled up to clear the line of trees at the south side of the airfield, the gunners opened up a withering fire, '. . . the hail of light flak and machine gun fire showered around us, the red points of the tracer rounds came flying by. I pushed the aircraft yet lower,' Unger later recorded.

Unteroffizier Schumacher, piloting another of the low-flying Dorniers, watched the bombs from the leading aircraft ram into the hangars: 'Other bombs were bouncing down the runway like rubber balls. Hell was let loose. Then the bombs began their work of destruction. Three hangars collapsed like matchwood. Explosion followed explosion, flames leapt into the sky. It seemed as if my aircraft was grabbed by some giant. Pieces of metal and stones clattered against the fuselage; something thudded into my back armour and splinters of glass flew. There was a smell of phosphorous and smouldering cables.'

The low-flying Dorniers delivered a devastatingly accurate attack on Kenley, but in doing so they too suffered heavily. One of the bombers crashed immediately beside the airfield. Another Dornier was hit and set on fire, two more had engines knocked out and in one the pilot was mortally wounded and the navigator had to take the controls. The four

Low-level engagement over Surrey

After their destructive low-altitude attack on Kenley airfield on 18 August, the Dorniers of 9./*Kampfgeschwader* 76 came under attack from the Hurricanes of No 111 Squadron. As he swept past the airfield Sergeant Harry Newton caught sight of one of the low-flying Dorniers and swung into a firing position. The bomber, piloted by *Unteroffizier* Günther Unger, had already had one engine knocked out by Flak. Newton saw tracer rounds coming back at him from his intended victim, but thought it looked a puny defence: I thought, "You've got one gun, I've got eight - you don't stand a chance!" Newton lined up on the Dornier and fired a burst at it, but saw his tracers going over the bomber's starboard wing.

As Günther Unger's Dornier left the target it came under attack from a Hurricane flown by Sergeant Harry Newton of No 111 Squadron, here depicted. As Newton ran in behind his intended victim an accurate burst from the Dornier's rear gunner, Unteroffizier Franz Bergmann, set the fighter on fire. Newton was lucky to escape with his life.

Then the German gunner, *Unteroffizier* Franz Bergmann, got in an accurate burst and his rounds slammed into the Hurricane's engine and fuel tanks.

Harry Newton continued: 'I thought, Just a slight correction and I've got him! But just at that moment he got me, because my cockpit seemed to burst into flames . . . But I was so annoyed at the thought of that Dornier getting away that I put my hand back into the flames, groped for the stick, made my correction and then loosed off a long burst in the direction of where I thought the Dornier was.'

Newton pulled his Hurricane into an almost vertical climb to gain altitude to bale out. To protect his eyes he kept them tightly closed, while around him the flames were burning through the three pairs of gloves, the flying suit and trousers he was wearing. In the climb the Hurricane's speed fell away rapidly, then the engine cut out. Newton slammed the stick forwards and at the same time clambered out of the cockpit and pulled his ripcord. "At that moment I opened my eyes, in time to see the tail of my Hurricane flash past my right ear, about a foot away. The next thing I knew the parachute had opened and the ground was coming up to meet me."

The bomber crew watched the blazing enemy fighter pull up and its pilot fall clear. There was no time to gloat over their fallen enemy, however, for the Dornier had suffered further damage during Newton's final despairing burst. The bomber made it to the coast, but soon afterwards the remaining engine began to lose power and Unger was forced to ditch the machine. The crew were rescued after three hours in the water, close to death from exposure, by a German patrol boat.

Brought together with his former enemies by the author, Harry Newton (centre) shows how he ran in to attack Unger's Dornier to Günther Unger (left) and Franz Bergmann (right), the rear gunner who shot Newton down.

This much-published photograph depicts a falling Dornier Do 17, but most often it comes without collateral details. In fact, this aircraft of I./KG 76 was shot down by Pilot Officer Alan Eckford flying a Hurricane of No 32 Squadron during the high-level engagement over Kenley on 18 August. It is seen going down in a shallow dive with the starboard engine on fire, and it would crash near Oxted in Surrey.

Left: Oberfeldwebel Wilhelm Lautersack, the above mentioned Dornier's flight engineer/rear gunner, and another crewman baled out and was taken prisoner.

Brought together by the author, Alan Eckford (right) and Wilhelm Lautersack had a cordial meeting at the RAF Museum at Hendon in 1979.

remaining Dorniers had suffered lesser amounts of damage. Then the Hurricanes of No 111 Squadron pounced on the raiders. They immediately finished off the bomber on fire and inflicted further damage on the others.

While this was happening, the high-altitude raiding forces bombed Kenley and Biggin Hill. During their withdrawal, they and their escorts were engaged by six fresh squadrons of Spitfires and Hurricanes which fought a running battle almost up to the French coast. By the end of the engagement the *Luftwaffe* had lost twenty-one aircraft. RAF Fighter Command lost seventeen fighters in air combat, and five more destroyed on the ground.

Kenley had been hit hard during the attack, which wrecked three of its four hangars and left the landing ground badly cratered; its fighters had to be diverted to other airfields, until troublesome craters had been filled in and several unexploded bombs made safe. By the next day, however, the airfield would again be fully operational. Although it had been attacked by sixty bombers, the airfield at Biggin Hill suffered remarkably little damage and it was able to continue operations.

Even as the raiders were streaming back to their bases after the first major attack of the day, the forces allocated to the second wave were airborne and heading for their targets. One hundred and nine Ju 87 Stukas drawn from *Sturzkampfgeschwader* 3 and 77 were heading for the airfields at Gosport, Ford and Thorney Island and the radar station at Poling, escorted by more than a hundred and fifty Bf 109s. Again the British coastal radar stations located the raiders well out to sea, and sixty-eight Spitfires and Hurricanes from five squadrons had been scrambled.

The British squadrons were moving into position to intercept as the vanguard of the raiders crossed the coast. Standing sentry on the esplanade at Bognor, Private Arthur Sindall of the Royal Army Service Corps gazed in awe at the German bombers passing overhead.

Continued on page 58

Hauptmann Joachim Roth's Dornier lying burned out in a field near Kenley, after having been set on fire by the airfield's ground defences, then finished off by Hurricanes of No 111 Squadron. All five crewmen suffered wounds and were taken prisoner.

Smoke from the fires at the Kenley airfield, photographed from Coulsdon two miles to the north-east.

Above left: A Hurricane of No 615 Squadron damaged during the attack on Kenley. The unit lost four aircraft destroyed on the ground during the attack on 18 August.

Hangars wrecked at Kenley during the combined high- and low-level attack on 18 August.

BATTLE of BRITAIN

This Spitfire I, N3024 'PR-H', of 609 Squadron, was lost near Weymouth on 14 August whilst being flown by Flg Off Henry 'Mac' Goodwin. Scrambled in the wake of the devastating surprise raid on Middle Wallop by Ju 88s of 1./LG 1, Goodwin (who had claimed three kills in the previous two days) headed south and simply disappeared. Flying alone, he was almost certainly 'bounced' by enemy fighters, for a Spitfire was seen to crash into the sea off Boscombe Pier, in Dorset, a short while later. The pilot succeeded in baling out, but no trace of him could be found. Ten days later, 'Mac' Goodwin's body was washed ashore on the Isle of Wight.
This photograph shows a mission-ready N3024, and its groundcrew, at Middle Wallop in early August. Parked behind 'PR-H' is Spitfire I, L1096 'PR-G', which survived its long spell with No 609 Sqn, and was later passed on to the Fleet Air Arm.

Sgt Basil Whall (left) flew with No 602 Squadron and was credited with six victories and two shared during the battle. He was killed in action on 7 October 1940.

A Junkers Ju 87 dive-bomber shot down by Basil Whall on 18 August 1940.

Left and below: Spitfires of No 609 Squadron photographed early in the Battle, probably when the unit was operating from Warmwell as part of No 10 Group.

Plt Off Robert Doe of No 234 Squadron, left, was credited with the destruction of a Bf 109 on 18 August. His total score while flying Spitfires was 11 enemy aircraft destroyed and two shared destroyed. In September 1940, he transferred to a Hurricane squadron and shot down three more enemy aircraft. He survived the war.

Junkers Ju 87

The Junkers Ju 87 'Stuka' was the main dive-bomber type operated by the *Luftwaffe* during the Battle. It carried a crew of two: pilot, wireless-operator/rear gunner. Cruising speed in formation was 241 km/h (150 mph) with a maximum speed of 383 km/h (238 mph). It was armed with two 7.9 mm machine guns mounted in the wings firing forward and one firing rearwards. The normal bomb load was one 250 kg (550 lb) bomb under the fuselage and two 50 kg (110 lb) bombs under each wing.

These two close-ups of the main bombing mechanism used by the Ju 87 show the arm which swung downwards prior to bomb release. As the aircraft carried out its near vertical attack dive and released its fuselage bomb, the radius arm swung the bomb cleanly away from the aircraft to prevent it striking the propeller. This machine carries the emblem of 3./St.G. 2, a black eagle atop an iron cross on a yellow shield inside a yellow circle which was the arms of the city of Breslau where the Staffel was formed.

Ju 87 of I./StG 2. The emblem below the cockpit was the unit's badge, depicting the Scottish terrier belonging to the commander, Major Hubertus Hitschhold.

A group of interested spectators look on as RAF officers examine one of four Ju 87 Bs of 3./St.G. 2 which were shot down during an attack on Tangmere airfield on 16 August 1940.

'Poor old Biggin caught a packet. . .'

'Friday, 30th August. Poor old Biggin caught a packet that day. We were sitting at tea in the Mess when the loud speaker piped up and said "Take cover! Enemy aircraft approaching the aerodrome." We tore to the nearest shelter but nothing happened so presently we forgathered again and went on with tea. Twice more the same thing happened. When it happened a fourth time we slowly got up and strolled outside and watched seven Blenheims flying along in line astern about a mile to the south.

'All of a sudden the leading "Blenheim" did a quick turn to starboard and started a dive at us. We were in the shelter like greased lightning and a few seconds later there was a noise like an express train approaching and WHHOOMP – a fourpenny one landed in the road thirty yards away. I really thought that my last hour had come . . .

'When all of the "Whoomping" had finished we came out to see what was what. Several buildings had been hit, and one bomb had landed on a concrete shelter and killed about thirty troops including some WAAF. Most of 79 [Squadron] had an amazing escape. At the time of the warning they were getting into the Humber station wagon to go across to dispersal. They were just passing behind 32's hangar when the WAAF driver perceived what was happening, stopped and told then to go into a shelter which was about 10 yards away. The last of them (there were about ten in the wagon) had just got down inside when a bomb landed alongside the Humber, lifted it bodily seventy feet into the air and dropped it through the roof of our hangar where it landed on the concrete floor upside down.'

Michael Crossley's Diary

On 18 August the airfield at Biggin Hill came under attack. Afterwards Sergeant Elizabeth Mortimer, a WAAF armourer, was awarded the Military Medal for her work to make safe several unexploded bombs scattered around on the airfield.

'Their immaculate formation, wing-tip to wing-tip a kind of airborne Trooping of the Colour, engendered a grudging admiration. Their black and white crosses were all too clearly visible on the underside of the wings' he recalled.

Oberleutnant Julius Neumann of *Jagdgeschwader* 27, flying one of the Bf 109 escorts, remembered: 'I saw some small specks emerging from the patchy haze to the north: British fighters! I alerted my *Staffel*, then swung round to engage." But the Messerschmitts were too late to prevent eighteen Hurricanes of Nos 43 and 601 Squadrons punching their way through to one of the dive-bomber formations. Flight Lieutenant Frank Carey, leading the attack, fired a long burst into one of the Stukas and saw it go down in flames. Pilot Officer Clifford Gray attacked another and saw it begin to belch flames from the underside of the fuselage. Even so the dive-bomber continued on, so he closed to short range and gave it a 5-second burst. There was a bright explosion, then his victim fell into a steep dive and crashed near Nutbourne.

Through the corner of his eye, *Oberleutnant* Johannes Wilhelm glimpsed three of four British fighters come roaring past his Stuka. He had no time to see where they went next, however, for he was concentrating on holding position in formation and observing the target through the window in the floor of the cabin. He was just about to push the bomber into its near-vertical attack dive, when to one side of him a Stuka burst into flames and slid out of the formation. But still he held position. Then came a sudden loud crash from his engine and the aircraft began to shudder. Oil came streaming back over the cabin, blotting out everything outside. More disconcerting still, the cockpit began to fill with smoke: the aircraft was on fire. Wilhelm turned the Stuka on to its back and shouted *"Raus! (Get out!)"* to his gunner. The pilot slid back his canopy, then a gout of hot engine oil struck him in the face and almost blinded him. One after the other, the two men released their straps and fell clear of the stricken dive-bomber.

A Stuka Ju 87 B of 3./St.G 2 is seen possibly at St. Malo in France in August 1940. Although allocated its own Scottish terrier badge with the disc in yellow, the Staffel colour, 3./St.G 2 also had an alternate badge featuring the coat of arms of the city of Breslau, as shown in the photographs above. Note the generally weathered appearance. In the scene above, the machine is shown with its camouflage of foliage still in place and fully armed for its next mission. Note the individual aircraft's letter 'H' painted on the starboard wheel spat.

As other Stukas dived to attack their targets, the Hurricanes followed. Contrary to what several accounts have stated, a Stuka was almost invulnerable to fighter attack during its dive. Then its speed was controlled by the underwing dive brakes. Frank Carey told this writer: 'In the dive they were very difficult to hit, because in a fighter, one's speed built up so rapidly that one went screaming past him. But he couldn't dive for ever . . .'

Oberleutnant Otto Schmidt had just released his bombs on the hangars at Thorney Island, and was pulling out of the dive when something caught his eye to the rear: an enemy fighter, looming large. Then he realised why his gunner had not opened fire - the unfortunate man was collapsed lifeless in his seat. In concentrating on his dive attack, Schmidt had not noticed that his own aircraft had been hit. He pushed his Stuka into a screaming side-slip and the British fighter shot past.

Hauptmann Herbert Meisel, commander of I. Gruppe of Sturzkampfgeschwader 77, was killed during the attack on Thorney Island.

The final moments of a Ju 87 that crashed at West Broyle near Chichester on 18 August. Both crew members were killed.

Above: Oberleutnant Otto Schmidt of St.G 77 returned from Thorney Island with a dead rear gunner.

Fires burning at the Naval Air Station at Ford following the destructive attack by dive-bombers.

A Luftwaffe post-strike photograph showing the extent of the fires at Ford.

Squadron Leader Derek Boitel-Gill led the Spitfires of No 152 Squadron to attack the dive-bombers as they came away from their targets.

At her home at Nutbourne, close to the airfield at Thorney Island and right under the Stuka's approach path, housewife Amelia Sop, was sheltering under the stairs eating her lunch. From outside she could hear the whines of diving aircraft, the clatter of machine gun fire and the bangs of exploding shells and guns. Then her ear caught a different note – that of people shouting. Cautiously she made her way to the kitchen window and peeped outside, and then burst out laughing at the incongruous scene that greeted her. Her next-door neighbour's eight-year old son was standing on the top of the garden shed cheering on the British fighters, while his mother stood beside the shed shrieking at him to come down and get under cover. To shield her from the shell fragments, cartridge cases and spent rounds raining down from above, the woman held her white apron over her head!

As the raiders pulled away from their targets the remaining British squadrons charged into the mêlée. The 25-mile-long strip of coastline between Bognor and Gosport became transformed into a turmoil as more than three hundred aircraft from both sides, twisted and turned in combat, each side desperately endeavouring to bring guns to bear or to evade being fired upon.

Flying over the Isle of Wight, Flight Lieutenant Derek Boitel-Gill ordered the eleven Spitfires of No 152 Squadron into line astern and led them into the thick of the fighting. He picked out a gaggle of dive-bombers making its way to the south, fired a 4-second burst at one of them and saw it go straight into the sea. Pilot Officer Eric Marrs followed closely behind his leader: 'We dived after them and they went down to 100 feet above the water. Then followed a running chase out to sea. The evasive action they took was to throttle back and do steep turns to right and left, so that we would not be able to follow them and would overshoot. There were, however, so many of them that if one was shaken off the tail of one there was always another to sit on.' Marrs fired at several of the dive-bombers and saw one strike the sea streaming burning petrol from its port wing. 'When I had finished my ammunition I turned away and found an Me 109 sitting on my tail. As I turned, it fired a burst in front of me. I could see the tracer and seemed to fly straight through it. I was not hit, however, and ran for home as it was senseless staying without ammunition.'

During this engagement the *Luftwaffe* lost twenty-four aircraft, while Fighter Command lost five. A further twenty British aircraft were destroyed on the ground at Ford and Gosport, but none of these belonged to Fighter Command. Although the Stukas suffered serious losses, in each case they had hit their targets hard. The airfield at Ford would be out of action for several weeks.

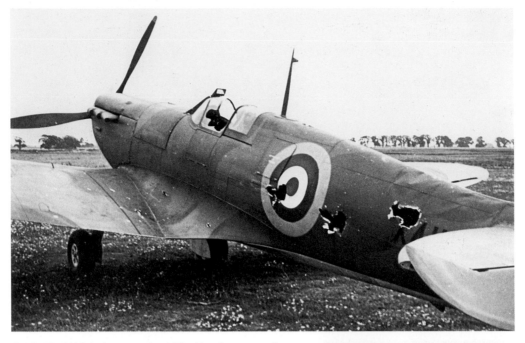

Spitfire X, 4110, had an operational life of less than twenty-five minutes! Delivered to No 602 Squadron at Westhampnett on the morning of 18 August, there was no time even to paint the squadron letters on the brand-new fighter before Flight Lieutenant Dunlop Urie took it into action over Bognor. Urie came under attack from a Bf 109, his aircraft was hit and he suffered leg wounds. The pilot landed the aircraft, but its back was broken and it never flew again.

Dunlop Urie, his feet bandaged, waiting to be taken to hospital after the action.

During the late afternoon the *Luftwaffe* launched its third major attack of the day: fifty-eight Dorniers of *Kampfgeschwader* 2 and fifty-one Heinkels of *Kampfgeschwader* 53 made for the fighter airfields at Hornchurch and North Weald, respectively. Escorting the bombers were one hundred and fifty Messerschmitts. On the British side, fifteen squadrons of Spitfires and Hurricanes scrambled to intercept.

As the German formations approached the coast, Nos 32, 54, 56 and 501 Squadrons closed in to engage. Flying Officer Innes Westmacott of No 56 Squadron, flying a Hurricane, recalled sighting the enemy: 'We had to go up through a bit of cloud and suddenly we saw them. I must say I gulped a bit! It looked an enormous raid.' Squadron Leader 'Minnie' Manton, leading the squadron, split his force into four and ordered three sections to go for the bombers while he and his section moved into position to hold off the Bf 110 escorts. Manton succeeded in getting on to the tail of one of the escorts and saw his rounds striking home. The Messerschmitt dived away to the south trailing glycol from a punctured radiator.

Meanwhile, Westmacott was having troubles of his own from other escorts. 'There were a lot of Messerschmitt 110s about and they all seemed to be picking on me! Whichever way I turned there seemed to be one shooting at me. I made for the cover of a small cloud. Unfortunately the cloud was too small and I kept on popping out of it, to find the Messerschmitts flying round outside. I had a shower of tracer about my ears . . . No friends were in sight and it was clear I had to get away fast.' Westmacott rolled his Hurricane on to its back and pulled it into a near-vertical dive. The needle of his airspeed indicator edged above 350 mph – equivalent to a true airspeed of over 450 mph – and the rush of the air coming past the canopy almost drowned the engine noise. The aircraft's controls felt as if they had been locked solid. With the sea rushing up to meet him, Westmacott hauled on the stick and almost blacked out. He prayed that the machine would hold together. It did, and the ferocity of his dive shook off his pursuers.

While other Hurricanes kept the escorts busy, Flying Officer 'Squeak' Weaver of No 56 Squadron was able to move in for an attack on one of the bombers. He singled out the left-hand Heinkel at the rear of the formation and fired a 10-second burst into it, then had to break away violently to avoid a Bf 110 closing on him from behind.

The Heinkel that Weaver had hit was flown by *Leutnant* Walter Leber of *Kampfgeschwader* 53. From his cockpit Leber saw nothing of the attack; the first he knew of it was the shout from his gunners that fighters were coming in, then a rattle as they opened up with their machine guns. The German pilot saw tracers streaking back from the guns of the Heinkels around him. Seconds later the temperature gauge of his starboard engine began to rise rapidly towards the danger mark: the cooling system had been hit. Leber feathered the propeller and shut the engine down. He struggled to keep up with the formation, but from the start it was a losing battle, and the Heinkel soon began to drop back. The lone bomber was a 'sitting duck' and it was not long before British fighters arrived to take advantage of the fact. Pilot Officer 'John Willie' Hopkin of No 54 Squadron ran in and fired a long 9-second burst into the bomber, knocking out its other engine and wounding three of the crew. Leber took his bomber down and made a crash landing on Foulness Island.

As the German formations moved inland, the perfidious British weather intervened. It would protect the targets more effectively than any man-made defence: a blanket of low cloud, approaching on a north-westerly breeze, drifted in to conceal the two British fighter airfields. The raiders were forced to turn around and head for home.

On the way out the raiders faced further sharp actions. Squadron Leader Peter Townsend, leading the thirteen Hurricanes of No 85 Squadron, tried to attack the bombers but found his path blocked by the escorts. He fired at a Bf 110 and saw it spiral away.

Sergeant John Etherington of No 17 Squadron, flying a Hurricane, also had problems during that particular engagement. 'It was a proper mix-up. I was going in one direction and the other squadrons came from the opposite direction. I attacked a Messerschmitt 110 and almost collided with a British fighter attacking the same aircraft. Someone had a go at me – I saw tracer coming past – I did not hang around to find out who it was. I had a couple of bursts at a 109, then it was all over. One moment the air was full of aircraft blazing away at each other and the next the sky was empty, almost like a dream.'

The *Luftwaffe* lost fourteen aircraft during this engagement; the Royal Air Force lost nine.

An armourer remembers

Those who flew during the Battle of Britain were utterly dependent upon the skill, the enthusiasm and the determination of those who prepared and repaired their aircraft. Representing the men and women who played such an essential part in winning the Battle, yet who never left the ground, is armourer Fred Tandy. The armourer's task during the Battle was to ensure that when a pilot had an enemy aircraft in his gunsight and pressed the firing button, the battery of guns performed the final act in the long chain of events between the order to take-off, and the destruction of an enemy aircraft. Fred Tandy recalled the task of re-arming of the Spitfire's eight .303-in Browning machine guns:

'I joined No 616 Squadron with Spitfire Is at Leconfield in January 1940, as an AC 1 armourer straight out of training. We were young and very keen and whenever there was an aircraft available we used to practice re-arming again and again to try to reduce the time needed. Initially it took a team of four armourers about twenty minutes to carry out this task. Then somebody worked out a way of using a canvas loop to pull the first round of the new ammunition belt through the breech of the gun; this was important because it meant we could now re-arm the Spitfire without having to remove the top covers from the gun bays. As a result of continual practice, and with twelve covers to remove instead of the original twenty, we cut the original twenty-minute re-arming time down by more than half.

'By the time of the Battle of Britain, re-arming had become a slick operation. As the Spitfire taxied in after its sortie, we armourers would be watching the canvas strips doped over the gun ports: if these had been blown off it meant the guns had been fired and re-arming was necessary. If this was the case and the aircraft was required to fly again immediately, the team of armourers would be waiting at the dispersal. Each man carried one ammunition box loaded with 300 rounds of .303-in ammunition under each arm. During the Battle it was usual to load two of the guns with armour-piercing ammunition, two with incendiary and four guns with ball ammunition; four out of the last 25 rounds in each box of ball ammunition were tracer, to give the pilot an indication that he was nearly out.

'Even before the propeller had stopped there would be two armourers under each wing, busily undoing the scores of half-turn Dzus fasteners securing the gun panels and ammunition box covers. Once these covers were off, the next step was to have a quick look into the breech mechanism of each gun, to check that there had been no stoppage and that the gun was serviceable: if the breech block was stopped in the rear position, it meant that the pilot had ceased fire; if it was stopped in the forward position, it meant that he had run out of ammunition; if there had been a stoppage

Aircraftman First Class Fred Tandy, (right), describes his work during the Battle.

the breech would usually be in the forward position, with a live round "up the spout".'

'Unless the gun was unserviceable, the breech mechanism would be pulled to the rear position, if it was not there already. The belts from the partially used ammunition boxes could be pulled clear, and the boxes themselves could be removed and placed on the ground. Now the guns were safe and one armourer on each side would start to swab out the gun barrels from the front, to clean away the crumbs of burnt cordite.

'Meanwhile the second armourer in the pair would be clicking the full ammunition boxes into place from underneath the wing, and threading the canvas straps round the first round in each one through the feed ways. With a firm pull on each one in turn, he would bring the first round in each new box up against the feed stops. Then he would cock the gun, which brought the first round out of the belt on to the face of the breech block and at the same time released the canvas loop which could then be pulled clear.

'The armourer would look up into the gun from underneath to check that the round had actually fed on to the face of the breech block, then press the manual release to bring the block forwards to feed the round into the chamber. Now, the only essential task remaining was to re-fit the gun and ammunition box covers to the underside of the wing.

'If there was time before the next take-off we would dope pieces of fabric over the firing ports, to keep the heat in and prevent the guns freezing up at high altitude. To save time during the Battle of Britain, we sometimes used ordinary medical sticking plaster for this purpose. If the grass was wet the Spitfire was notorious for throwing up mud and water on to the undersides of the wings during the take-off run. To prevent this moisture getting into the gun bays via the link and cartridge case ejector slots, we would dope pieces of newspaper over them.

'In 1940 there was a tremendous sense of "belonging" to one's fighter squadron. Three ground crewmen were allocated to each Spitfire: a fitter, a rigger and an armourer; and it was a matter of great distress if anything happened to "their" pilot. Yet in spite of quite severe losses in pilots, morale was sky-high. At Kenley, during the Battle of Britain, we could see the combats being fought overhead; we could see the enemy aircraft being shot down and we knew that we on the ground had our own vital part to play in bringing this about. For a young lad of nineteen, they were stirring times.'

Petrol for running private cars was hard to come by in wartime. Here RAF personnel are seen removing petrol from a Ju 88 of KG 54 that crash-landed near Tangmere, into a private car belonging to one of them. Such misuse of captured material was against the law, but it was sufficiently unusual for those in authority to turn a blind eye. Note that the Swastika emblem has been cut away from the both sides of the tail fin, for souvenirs.

During the three major attacks and numerous smaller ones on 18 August, the *Luftwaffe* lost sixty-nine aircraft destroyed or damaged beyond repair. Fighter Command lost thirty-one fighters destroyed or damaged beyond repair in air combat, and seven destroyed on the ground. A further twenty-nine British aircraft were destroyed on the ground, none of them fighters, during the attacks on airfields.

During that day eleven British fighter pilots were killed and nineteen wounded. *Luftwaffe* aircrew losses amounted to ninety-four killed, twenty-five wounded and forty taken prisoner. Thus it cost the *Luftwaffe* nearly two aircraft for each British fighter destroyed, and five *Luftwaffe* aircrew killed, wounded or taken prisoner for each RAF fighter pilot killed or wounded. The loss of pilots has often been cited as the factor limiting Fighter Command's operations during the battle. But, even allowing for the greater strength of the attacking force, the German losses in trained aircrew were the more serious and damaging.

Both sides greatly exaggerated the number of enemy aircraft they had destroyed during the action on 18 August. The *Luftwaffe* (with 142 enemy aircraft claimed destroyed in the air and on the ground) overclaimed by just over three-to-one. The Royal Air Force (with 123 enemy planes claimed destroyed by fighters and 15 by anti-aircraft guns) overclaimed by two-to-one.

Squadron Leader Peter Townsend, centre, leaning on walking stick, pictured with pilots of No 85 Squadron. Townsend had been shot down on 31 August, when he was forced to bale out of his Hurricane after being wounded in his left foot.

Squadron Leader Peter Townsend (right) with his ground crew. His Hurricane has been rearmed, as seen by the canvas patches over the gun ports, and the external starter is plugged in.

The King awarding the DSO and the DFC to Squadron Leader Joseph Kayll, Hurricane pilot and commander of No 615 Squadron, at Kenley. In the background on the left stands Air Chief Marshal Dowding.

Following the heavy losses suffered that day, the Junkers Ju 87s took little further part in the Battle of Britain. The dive-bombers represented the most effective anti-shipping force available to the *Luftwaffe*, and they needed to be conserved so they could counter the Royal Navy if the planned German invasion got under way. Also, following the savage mauling suffered by the Dornier 17s of 9./*Kampfgeschwader* 76 during its low-level attack on Kenley – four aircraft destroyed and the other five all damaged – the unit would make no more such attacks.

During this and previous actions, the Messerschmitt Bf 110, like the RAF's Defiant, was shown to be vulnerable when confronted by enemy single-seaters. But whereas the Defiant represented a small proportion of Fighter Command's front-line strength, the Bf 110 constituted about a quarter of the German fighter force. With the scale of the bomber attacks already being limited by the number of fighters available to escort them, the German High Command was loath to reduce its fighter force still further. It was decided that the Bf 110s should play a reduced part in the fighting.

Most far-reaching of the new German measures was Göring's decision that in future a proportion of the escorts was to stick closely to the bombers. Fighters assigned to the close escort of bombers had strict orders that on no account were they to leave the vicinity of their charges; they were allowed to go into action only if the bombers they were protecting came under direct attack from enemy fighters. Ideally there would also be a fighter sweep through the area to break up the British attacks before they could develop, but often this was not the case.

Of course, these decisions on the German side were not immediately known to Fighter Command's leaders, Dowding and Park. They knew only that during the previous eight days' heavy fighting the British squadrons had suffered serious losses. To reduce pilot losses, Air Vice Marshal Park ordered that whenever possible fighter controllers were to vector their charges against the German formations over land, rather than over the sea where those who came down in the water might be lost.

Scramble!

To the pilots of Fighter Command the code-word 'Scramble' meant to 'Get airborne as rapidly as possible'. The men ran to their aircraft as if their lives depended on it. Because they did. Each thirty seconds' delay in getting airborne meant about 1,000 feet the pilots would not have when they needed it most – when they met the enemy. Squadron Leader Don Macdonell, commanding No 64 Squadron with Spitfires, described the scene:

'When we were at readiness the pilots would be relaxing at the dispersal area – reading, chatting, playing cards. Each Flight had a separate crew room, so no pilot was too far from his Spitfire. I would be out of my office, wearing flying kit and Mae West, with the Flight I was to lead on that day. Each pilot's parachute was laid out on the seat of his aircraft, with the straps laid over the armour plating at the back of the cockpit.

'Every time the telephone rang there would be a ghastly silence. The orderly would answer it and often one would hear something like: "Yes, Sir … yes, Sir … Yes Sir … Sergeant Smith wanted on the phone." And everyone would breathe again.

'If the call was for the squadron to scramble, the orderly would shout "SCRAMBLE!" at the top of his voice and every pilot would dash for his aircraft.

'By the time I reached my Spitfire the mechanic would have started the engine. He got out of the cockpit and I got in, and he helped me strap into my parachute. Then he passed the seat straps and helped me fasten them. When I gave the thumbs up he would shut the side door, jump to the ground and run round in front of the port wing. Meanwhile I tightened my various straps, pulled on my helmet and plugged in the R/T lead. After checking that the engine was running properly, I would wave the ground crew to pull away the chocks, open the throttle, and move forward out of my blast pen.

'After a fast taxi across the grass to the take-off position I would line up, open the throttle wide and begin my take-off run. The rest of my pilots followed me as fast as they could. The whole thing, from the scramble order to the last aircraft leaving the ground, took about a minute and a half.

'As soon as we were off the ground and climbing, I would inform operations "Freema Squadron airborne" ['Freema' was No 64 Squadron's radio callsign]. The Sector Controller would come back and tell me where he wanted me to go and at what altitude. While the squadron was forming up, I would climb in a wide spiral at low boost, until everyone was in place. Then I would open up to a high throttle setting to get to altitude as fast as possible. In the spiral climb I would always edge to the north; the enemy formations always came from the south or south-east, and it was important to avoid climbing below the enemy's fighter cover. As well as keeping watch for the enemy, I would be watching the station-keeping of my squadron. If anyone was beginning to straggle I would throttle back a little.'

The pace of operations during the Battle left pilots exhausted and it became necessary to snatch sleep whenever possible. Here pilots of No 65 Squadron are seen at '30 minutes available' at Rochford.

Providing Close Escort for the Bomber Formations

'Sometimes we were ordered to provide close escort for a bomber formation, which I loathed. It gave the bomber crews the feeling they were being protected, and it might have deterred some of the enemy pilots. But for us fighter pilots it was very bad. We needed the advantages of altitude and speed so we could engage the enemy on favourable terms. As it was, the British fighters had the initiative of when and how to attack.

'The Heinkels cruised at about 4,000 metres [13,000 feet] at about 300 km/h [190 mph]. On close escort we flew at about 370 km/h [230 mph], weaving from side to side to keep station on them. We needed to maintain speed; otherwise the Bf 109s would have taken too long to accelerate to fighting speed if we were bounced by Spitfires.

'I hated having to fly direct escort. We had to stay with the bombers until our formation came under attack. When we saw the British fighters approaching we would want to accelerate to engage them. But our commander would call "Everybody stay with the bombers." We handed to the enemy the initiative of when and how they would attack us. Until they did, we had to stay close to the bombers, otherwise their people would complain and there would be recriminations when we got back.'

Oberleutnant Hans Schmoller-Haldy, Bf 109 pilot, *Jagdgeschwader* 54

Following the seven days' ferocious fighting up to dusk on the 18th, there were six days of poor weather which effectively prevented large scale air operations. During this lull Dowding decided to give the Defiant another chance: No 264 Squadron was ordered south, to Hornchurch. In an effort to prevent the type of fighter-versus-fighter combat which had proved so disastrous just over a month earlier, Park instructed his Sector controllers:

'The Defiants whenever practicable are to be detailed to attack the enemy bombers. They may also attack fighters that are attacking ground targets, but are not to be detailed to intercept fighter formations. Moreover the Defiants are not normally to be despatched to intercept raids beyond gliding distance of the coastline except the Thames estuary.'

When the *Luftwaffe* resumed its attack, on 24 August, there were further heavy raids on the Fighter Command airfields. Thus began a period of nearly two weeks of daily combat during which Fighter Command, and in particular No 11 Group, had to fight hard for its very existence. On the 24th the airfield at Manston was put out of action and had temporarily to be abandoned. On the 26th Kenley, Biggin Hill and Debden were all hit hard. On the 28th, in spite of the controllers' attempts to keep them clear of enemy fighters, the Defiants of No 264 Squadron were caught by Bf 109s and lost four shot down and three damaged out of twelve aircraft, without shooting down any enemy fighters. After that, the Defiants were relegated to night operations for good. On the final day of August there were heavy attacks on Croydon, Hornchurch and Biggin Hill.

September brought no immediate relief for Air Vice Marshal Park's hard-pressed squadrons. On each of the first six days there were large-scale actions round the fighter airfields. Factories producing aircraft were also hit, though without causing any serious fall in production. In the course of the fighting during the final two weeks of this period, from

The Defiants leave the day battle

'During the week we were at Hornchurch at the end of August we lost five pilots and nine gunners. The squadron commander, the squadron commander designate and both flight commanders were all killed or wounded.

'By midday on the 28th there were only two Defiants serviceable and I flew on the Squadron's last daylight patrol in the Hornchurch Sector. We took off and were being vectored towards thirty-plus enemy aircraft. But before we reached them the controller came up on the radio and said "I'm terribly sorry, old boy, but they've turned back. Return to base and Pancake [land]." I don't know how the other three felt, but I certainly knew that if the 'thirty plus had turned out to be Bf 109s we would have been in for an interesting time!

'On the next day the half-dozen aircraft that were made flyable took off from Hornchurch for Kirton-in-Lindsey in Lincolnshire. They were led by a twenty-year-old Pilot Officer, the senior officer on the squadron.'

Pilot Officer Desmond Hughes, Defiant pilot, No 264 Squadron

'I began to plot the raid approaching Biggin Hill ..."

'When we came on duty the whole operations room was hectic, a mass of activity. Every plotter around the table was marking out raids over Kent and Sussex, and over the Channel en route. The controller and others on the platform were frantically busy in radio contact with out squadrons. I took over a position plotting several raids in Kent and was kept particularly busy keeping up with the information passed to me. Enemy aircraft singly, or in squadrons or even larger numbers, were so numerous.

'I remember the strange feeling as I began to plot the raid approaching Biggin Hill. It came nearer and nearer, until the arrow I placed was immediately over the aerodrome. At the same time we could hear the bombs dropping, falling some distance away. Then as the sounds came nearer, the controller yelled for us to take cover. I remember I could see him talking over the R/T to our squadrons while he was sheltering under the desk. There was a huge bang and part of the operations room came crashing down. The glass screen on which we plotted our squadrons was smashed. Shattered glass was everywhere, it was in our hair and cut our stockings but no one was seriously hurt. The table protected us.

'All were strangely silent. Rather shocked, we straggled out over the debris and were told to go to our quarters.'

Aircraftwoman Elaine Lewis, aircraft plotter, Operations Room, Biggin Hill.

24 August to 6 September, Fighter Command lost 103 pilots killed and 128 wounded. With about 1,500 pilots in his Command, Dowding was losing them at a rate of about one-twelfth per week. During August 250 new pilots emerged from operational training units, but these inexperienced newcomers often fell as easy prey before they learned how to survive in battle.

In the latter half of August, the *Luftwaffe* began to mount night attacks on targets in England, in parallel with those by day. The night raids were far less accurate than those during the day and the raiders scattered their bombs over a wide area. On one of the first of these attacks, on 24 August, a few bombs unintentionally fell on London. That raid would have far-reaching consequences, for it would lead to a retaliatory attack by the Royal Air Force on Berlin. And the implications of that will be discussed later.

On 25 and 26 August the night raiders hit Birmingham. Then, on the nights of the 28th, 29th, 30th and 31st, Liverpool came under repeated attack from raiding forces of about 150 aircraft. The port came under further attack on the nights of 4th, 5th and 6th September.

If the night attacks were far less accurate than those by day, compensating for this was the relative invulnerability of the raiders during the hours of darkness. Few of the defending gun batteries had fire-control radar and even fewer RAF fighters carried airborne interception (AI) radar. And in any case, these first-generation equipments were crude and unreliable, and their operators had to learn to handle them from first principles. In contrast to the fierce battles being fought by day, by night it was unusual for a raider to be seen and very rare for one to be shot down.

During the opening phase of the Battle the *Luftwaffe* lost 629 aircraft and the Royal Air Force lost 385. This gave a loss ratio of 1.6:1 in favour of the Royal Air Force, which was rather less than during the earlier skirmishes but still one that was satisfactory to the defenders.

RAF Fighter Command had taken some hard knocks during this phase of the Battle but its ground infrastructure, though battered, was still functioning well. Although all the main airfields in No 11 Group had suffered damage, there was an efficient organisation to fill craters in the landing grounds. Only one airfield, at Manston, was put out of action for more than a

The recollections of an anti-aircraft gunner

'I remember the Battle of Britain as one almost continuous grind of carrying ammunition (two 56-lb cartridges in a 28-lb steel box, 140 pounds in all, one per man), changing gun barrels when they were worn down (1 ton between eight men, lifted nearly 5 feet) and long periods of duty. We worked bloody hard, with none of the glamour enjoyed by the fighter pilots.'

Gunner Peter Erwood, 75 Heavy Anti Aircraft Regiment, 3.7-in gun battery, Dover, Kent

few hours. Rarely could raiders catch RAF fighters on the ground: by the time the bombers arrived over an airfield, the fighter squadrons based there were usually airborne and well clear. Fighters able to fly, but not fight, were sent off on 'survival scrambles', to keep clear of the enemy and to return when the raiders had passed. Aircraft unable to fly were wheeled into the protective revetments or dispersed around the airfield, where they were hard to hit from the air. Despite the almost daily attacks on their airfields over a period of more than three weeks, thanks to these precautions, less than 20 RAF fighters were destroyed on the ground.

To provide warning to scramble its fighters in good time, Fighter Command relied on its coastal radar stations. The radars were attacked from the air, but they also proved difficult targets. From above the radar stations represented very small pin-point targets. The buildings containing their vital equipment were protected by revetments, and were impervious to anything but a direct hit. Only dive-bombing gave the accuracy necessary to hit such small targets, and we have seen the mauling the Ju 87s received when they operated over southern England. Although they looked fragile, the radar's openwork metal towers supporting the aerials presented a small area to blast pressure or fragmentation effects and few were knocked down. Despite several attacks on radar stations, only one was put out of action for more than a few hours.

From the *Luftwaffe* viewpoint, however, it now looked as if Fighter Command was on its last legs (see page 45 'An Intelligence Trap Awaiting the *Luftwaffe*'). If that assessment was

This photograph shows Bob Stanford Tuck (centre of photograph) and fellow pilots of 257 Squadron, posing in front of Tuck's Hurricane.

anywhere near accurate, now was the time for a series of bold lunges at targets close to Britain's heartland. That would put an end to the island nation's recalcitrance for once and for all.

THE ASSAULT ON THE AIRFIELDS - AIRCRAFT LOSSES

Date	Luftwaffe	RAF	Action
13 August	39	14	Heavy attacks on airfields.
14 August	18	9	Heavy attacks on airfields.
15 August	79	34	Heavy attacks on airfields.
16 August	44	27	Heavy attacks on airfields.
17 August	2	1	Little activity.
18 August	69	39	Heavy attacks on airfields.
19 August	4	5	Poor weather, little activity.
20 August	6	1	Poor weather, little activity.
21 August	12	4	Poor weather, little activity.
22 August	2	4	Poor weather, little activity.
23 August	4	1	Poor weather, little activity.
24 August	34	18	Day: heavy attacks on airfields. Night: some bombs hit London.
25 August	19	18	Day: attacks on airfields. Night: Birmingham attacked.
26 August	38	30	Day: heavy attacks on airfields. Night: Birmingham attacked.
27 August	9	6	Little activity.
28 August	28	13	Day: attacks on airfields. Night: Liverpool attacked.
29 August	18	10	Day: fighter sweeps. Night: Liverpool attacked.
30 August	36	24	Day: heavy attacks on airfields. Night: Liverpool attacked.
31 August	34	38	Day: heavy attacks on airfields. Night: Liverpool attacked.
1 September	11	13	Day: attacks on airfields. Night: Swansea and Bristol hit.
2 September	33	14	Day: attacks on airfields.
3 September	14	11	Day: attacks on airfields. Night: Liverpool attacked.
4 September	22	14	Day: attacks on airfields. Night: Liverpool attacked.
5 September	24	19	Day: attacks on airfields. Night: Liverpool attacked.
6 September	30	18	Day: attacks on Weybridge and Medway towns. Night: London docks hit.
TOTALS	**629**	**385**	

THE ATTACK ON LONDON CHAPTER 3

'In approaching the prospects for a successful air campaign . . . [against Great Britain] there is one conspicuously favourable factor which will tend to influence Germany's judgement and encourage her to hope for success, and that is the exposed position and vulnerability of London . . . Nothing that either France or ourselves can attack in Germany can have quite the immediate and decisive results that Germany may hope to gain by an overwhelming attack on London.'

MARSHAL OF THE ROYAL AIR FORCE, SIR EDWARD ELLINGTON, CHIEF OF THE AIR STAFF
SPEAKING BEFORE THE WAR

DURING the final week in August the Royal Air Force had begun attacking targets in Germany, notably Berlin, in retaliation for some stray bombs that had fallen on London. The move enraged Hitler, who now ordered a series of heavy attacks on the British capital by way of a reprisal.

The new phase in the bombardment began on 7 September. The morning and early afternoon were quiet, with only reconnaissance activity over southern England. It was a fine sunny day and that, in contrast with intensive action of the previous two weeks, made the silence yet more ominous. The uneasy calm ended shortly before 1600 hrs when the radar stations began passing plots on yet another large-scale attack building up over the Pas de Calais. The raiding force crossed the coast at 1616 hrs: some 350 bombers, escorted by more than 600 fighters, forming a huge phalanx of aircraft advancing relentlessly across Kent.

No 11 Group's controllers scrambled almost every available squadron but, ignorant of the raiders' objective, they deployed the fighters to meet yet another attack on airfields. Only four squadrons were in position to block an attack on London, and the powerful force of escorts brushed these aside with little difficulty. The targets were the dock areas to the east of the capital, each with its lines of warehouses stuffed with imported goods. The raiders delivered a series of concentrated attacks which started huge fires.

During its first pitched battle over and around the capital, Fighter Command did not really get to grips with the enemy. The *Luftwaffe* lost forty aircraft, the Royal Air Force lost twenty-one fighters destroyed and an unusually heavy loss of pilots – seventeen killed or seriously wounded.

After dark more than three hundred bombers returned to London, to deliver a follow-up attack on the dock areas. With little to fear from the defences, the bombers flew direct routes from their bases, converging on London from every direction between south-west to due east. The bombers arrived over the capital in ones and twos and the bombing continued for more than six hours, from 2210 hrs until 0430 hrs the following morning.

With their targets clearly marked by the fires started earlier in the day, the night raiders dropped their loads of high explosive and incendiary bombs to reinforce the fires and disrupt the work of the firefighters. By 1 am nine fires had grown so large that they merited the official description 'conflagration'. One of these, in the area around Quebec Yard in the Surrey Docks, continued spreading and it would grow into the fiercest single fire ever recorded in Britain. (In this context a 'conflagration' was defined as 'a major fire that was spreading and requiring more than one hundred pumps to bring it under control'; a 'major fire' was one that

Continued on page 80

Luftwaffe Units Deployed to Attack the United Kingdom, 7 September 1940

Note: *Luftwaffe* unit strength returns were compiled at ten-day intervals. This gives the return on 7 September, the last one issued before the decisive action on 5 September. The first figure gives aircraft serviceable; the second figure gives aircraft unserviceable.

LUFTFLOTTE 2, HQ BRUSSELS

LONG-RANGE BOMBERS

Kampfgeschwader 1

Stab	Heinkel He 111	5	2	Rosières-en-Santerre
I. Gruppe	Heinkel He 111	22	14	Montdidier, Clairmont
II. Gruppe	Heinkel He 111	23	13	Montdidier, Nijmegen
III. Gruppe	Junkers Ju 88	-	9	Rosières-en-Santerre

Kampfgeschwader 2

Stab	Dornier Do 17	6	0	Saint-Leger
I. Gruppe	Dornier Do 17	12	7	Cambrai
II. Gruppe	Dornier Do 17	20	11	Saint-Leger
III. Gruppe	Dornier Do 17	20	10	Cambrai

Kampfgeschwader 3

Stab	Dornier Do 17	5	1	Le Culot
I. Gruppe	Dornier Do 17	25	4	Le Culot
II. Gruppe	Dornier Do 17	23	4	Antwerp/Deurne
III. Gruppe	Dornier Do 17	19	9	Saint-Trond

Kampfgeschwader 4

Stab	Heinkel He 111	5	5	Soesterberg
I. Gruppe	Heinkel He 111	16	21	Soesterberg
II. Gruppe	Heinkel He 111	30	7	Eindhoven
III. Gruppe	Junkers Ju 88	14	16	Amsterdam/Schiphol

Kampfgeschwader 26

Stab	Heinkel He 111	3	3	Gilze-Rijen
I. Gruppe	Heinkel He 111	7	18	Moerbeke, Courtrai (operated from Wevelghem on 15 September)
II. Gruppe	Heinkel He 111	7	19	Gilze-Rijen

Kampfgeschwader 30

Stab	Junkers Ju 88	1	-	Brussels
I. Gruppe	Junkers Ju 88	1	9	Brussels
II. Gruppe	Junkers Ju 88	24	6	Gilze-Rijen

Kampfgeschwader 40

Stab	Fw 200	1	1	Bordeaux

Kampfgeschwader 53

Stab	Heinkel He 111	3	2	Lille
I. Gruppe	Heinkel He 111	19	4	Lille
II. Gruppe	Heinkel He 111	7	22	Lille
III. Gruppe	Heinkel He 111	4	15	Lille

Kampfgeschwader 76

Stab	Dornier Do 17	3	3	Cormeilles-en-Vexin
I. Gruppe	Dornier Do 17	19	7	Beauvais/Tille
II. Gruppe	Junkers Ju 88	21	6	Creil
III. Gruppe	Dornier Do 17	17	7	Cormeilles-en-Vexin

Kampfgeschwader 77

Stab	Junkers Ju 88	1	-	Laon
I. Gruppe	Junkers Ju 88	31	5	Laon
II. Gruppe	Junkers Ju 88	25	7	Asch
III. Gruppe	Junkers Ju 88	19	11	Laon

Kampfgruppe 126

	Heinkel He 111	26	7	Marx

DIVE-BOMBERS AND FIGHTER-BOMBERS

Sturzkampfgeschwader 1

Stab	Ju 87, Do 17	5	2	Saint-Pol
II. Gruppe	Junkers 87	29	14	Pas de Calais

Sturzkampfgeschwader 2

Stab	Ju 87, Do 17	9	2	Tramecourt
II. Gruppe	Junkers 87	22	5	Saint Omer, Saint-Trond

Lehr Geschwader 1

IV *Gruppe*	Junkers 87	28	14	Tramecourt

Lehr Geschwader 2

II. Gruppe	Bf 109	27	5	Saint Omer (fighter-bomber unit)

SINGLE-ENGINED FIGHTERS

Jagdgeschwader 1

Stab	Bf 109	3	1	Pas de Calais area

Jagdgeschwader 3

Stab	Bf 109	3	-	Samer
I. Gruppe	Bf 109	14	9	Samer
II. Gruppe	Bf 109	21	3	Samer
III. Gruppe	Bf 109	23	2	Desvres

Jagdgeschwader 26

Stab	Bf 109	3	1	Audembert
I. Gruppe	Bf 109	20	7	Audembert
II. Gruppe	Bf 109	28	4	Marquise
III. Gruppe	Bf 109	26	3	Caffiers

Jagdgeschwader 27

Stab	Bf 109	4	1	Etaples
I. Gruppe	Bf 109	27	6	Etaples
II. Gruppe	Bf 109	33	4	Montreuil
III. Gruppe	Bf 109	27	4	Sempy

Jagdgeschwader 51

Stab	Bf 109	4	1	Saint Omer
I. Gruppe	Bf 109	33	3	Saint Omer, Saint Inglevert
II. Gruppe	Bf 109	13	9	Saint Omer, Saint Inglevert
III. Gruppe	Bf 109	31	13	Saint Omer

Jagdgeschwader 52

Stab	Bf 109	1	1	Laon/Couvron
I. Gruppe	Bf 109	17	4	Laon/Couvron
II. Gruppe	Bf 109	23	5	Pas de Calais area
III. Gruppe	Bf 109	16	15	Pas de Calais area

Jagdgeschwader 53

Stab	Bf 109	2	-	Pas de Calais area
II. Gruppe	Bf 109	24	9	Wissant
III. Gruppe	Bf 109	22	8	Pas de Calais area

Jagdgeschwader 54

Stab	Bf 109	2	2	Holland
I. Gruppe	Bf 109	23	5	Holland
II. Gruppe	Bf 109	27	8	Holland
III. Gruppe	Bf 109	23	5	Holland

Jagdgeschwador 77

I. Gruppe	Bf 109	40	2	Pas de Calais area

TWIN-ENGINED FIGHTERS

Zerstoerergeschwader 2

Stab	Bf 110	-	1	Pas de Calais area
I. Gruppe	Bf 110	10	10	Amiens, Caen
II. Gruppe	Bf 110	10	18	Guyancourt/Caudran

Zerstoerergeschwader 26

Stab	Bf 110	3	-	Lille
I. Gruppe	Bf 110	14	19	Abbeville, Saint Omer
II. Gruppe	Bf 110	17	8	Crécy
III. Gruppe	Bf 110	17	8	Barley, Arques

Lehr Geschwader 1

V *Gruppe*	Bf 110	19	4	Ligescourt, Alencon
Erprobungsgruppe 210				
	Bf 109, Bf 110	17	9	Denain (fighter-bomber unit)

LONG-RANGE RECONNAISSANCE

Aufklärungsgruppe 22

1. *Staffel*	Do 17, Bf 110	9	4	Lille

Aufklärungsgruppe 122

1. *Staffel*	Junkers Ju 88	3	5	Holland
2. *Staffel*	Ju 88, He 111	9	1	Brussels/Millbrook
3. *Staffel*	Ju 88, He 111	10	1	Eindhoven
4. *Staffel*	Ju 88, He 111, Bf 110	9	4	Brussels
5. *Staffel*	Ju 88, He 111	11	-	Haute-Fountain

MARITIME RECONNAISSANCE AND MINE LAYING AIRCRAFT

Küstenfliegergruppe 106

1. *Staffel*	Heinkel 115	4	6	Brittany area
2. *Staffel*	Dornier 18	6	3	Brittany area
3. *Staffel*	Heinkel 115	6	3	Borkum

LUFTFLOTTE 3, HQ PARIS

LONG-RANGE BOMBERS

Lehr Geschwader 1

Stab	Junkers Ju 88	3	-	Orléans/Bricy
I. Gruppe	Junkers Ju 88	13	14	Orléans/Bricy
II. Gruppe	Junkers Ju 88	19	12	Orléans/Bricy
III. Gruppe	Junkers Ju 88	19	11	Chateaudun

Kampfgeschwader 27

Stab	Heinkel He 111	4	3	Tours
I. Gruppe	Heinkel He 111	13	22	Tours
II. Gruppe	Heinkel He 111	15	17	Dinard, Bourges
III. Gruppe	Heinkel He 111	13	7	Rennes

Kampfgeschwader 40

I. Gruppe	Fw 200	4	3	Bordeaux

Kampfgeschwader 51

Stab	Junkers Ju 88	-	1	Orly
I. Gruppe	Junkers Ju 88	13	20	Melun
II. Gruppe	Junkers Ju 88	17	17	Orly
III. Gruppe	Junkers Ju 88	27	7	Etampes

Kampfgeschwader 54

Stab	Junkers Ju 88	-	1	Evreux
I. Gruppe	Junkers Ju 88	18	12	Evreux
II. Gruppe	Junkers Ju 88	14	12	St André

Kampfgeschwader 55

Stab	Heinkel He 111	6	-	Villacoublay
I. Gruppe	Heinkel He 111	20	7	Dreux
II. Gruppe	Heinkel He 111	22	8	Chartres
III. Gruppe	Heinkel He 111	20	5	Villacoublay

Kampfgruppe 100

	Heinkel He 111	7	21	Vannes

Kampfgruppe 606

	Dornier Do 17	29	4	Brest, Cherbourg

Kampfgruppe 806

	Junkers Ju 88	18	9	Nantes, Caen

DIVE-BOMBERS

Sturzkampfgeschwader 3

Stab	Do 17, He 111	6	1	Brittany area
I. Gruppe	Junkers 87	34	3	Brittany area

SINGLE-ENGINED FIGHTERS

Jagdgeschwader 2

Stab	Bf 109	2	3	Beaumont-le-Roger
I. Gruppe	Bf 109	24	5	Beaumont-le-Roger
II. Gruppe	Bf 109	18	4	Beaumont-le-Roger
III. Gruppe	Bf 109	19	11	Le Havre

Jagdgeschwader 53

I. Gruppe	Bf 109	27	7	Brittany area

TWIN-ENGINED FIGHTERS
Zerstörergeschwader 76

Stab	Bf 110	2	2	
II. Gruppe	Bf 110	12	15	Le Mans, Abbeville
III. Gruppe	Bf 110	8	11	Laval

LONG-RANGE RECONNAISSANCE
Lehr Geschwader 2

7. *Staffel*	Bf 110	9	5

Aufklärungsgruppe 14

4. *Staffel*	Bf 110, Do 17	9	3	Normandy area

Aufklärungsgruppe 31

3. *Staffel*	Bf 110, Do 17	5	4	St Brieuc

Aufklärungsgruppe 121

3. *Staffel*	Ju 88, He 111	6	4	North-west France
4. *Staffel*	Ju 88, Do 17	5	8	Normandy

Aufklärungsgruppe 123

1. *Staffel*	Ju 88, Do 17	7	3	Paris area
2. *Staffel*	Ju 88, Do 17	8	2	Paris area
3. *Staffel*	Ju 88, Do 17	9	3	Buck

LUFTFLOTTE 5, HQ KRISTIANSUND, NORWAY
SINGLE-ENGINED FIGHTERS
Jagdgeschwader 77

II. Gruppe	Bf 109	35	9	Southern Norway

LONG-RANGE RECONNAISSANCE
Aufklärungsgruppe 22

2. *Staffel*	Dornier Do 17	5	4	Stavanger
3. *Staffel*	Dornier Do 17	5	4	Stavanger

Aufklärungsgruppe 120

1. *Staffel*	He 111, Ju 88	2	11	Stavanger

Aufklärungsgruppe 121

1. *Staffel*	He 111, Ju 88	2	5	Stavanger, Aalborg

MARITIME RECONNAISSANCE AND MINELAYING AIRCRAFT
Küstenfliegergruppe 506

1. *Staffel*	Heinkel 115	6	2	Stavanger
2. *Staffel*	Heinkel 115	5	3	Trondheim, Tromsö
3. *Staffel*	Heinkel 115	6	2	List

When German multi-engined bombers came under attack from RAF fighters, the raiders moved in close formation, as seen here from an He 111, to concentrate their defensive fire.

Heinkel He 111 of III./KG 53 piloted by Leutnant Walter Leber.

Right: Close-up of the Heinkel He 111, showing the excellent view from the observer's glazed position in the nose. The pilot, however, had a much reduced field of view from his position further to the rear.

Royal Air Force Fighter Command Units, 1800 hrs, 14 September 1940

First figure aircraft serviceable, second figure aircraft unserviceable

No 10 Group, HQ Box, Wiltshire

MIDDLE WALLOP SECTOR

238 Squadron	Hurricanes	17	1	Middle Wallop
609 Squadron	Spitfires	15	3	Middle Wallop
604 Squadron	Blenheims	5	14	Middle Wallop
	Beaufighters	-	1	Middle Wallop
Half 23 Squadron	Blenheims	6	-	Middle Wallop
152 Squadron	Spitfires	17	2	Warmwell
56 Squadron	Hurricanes	17	-	Boscombe Down

FILTON SECTOR

79 Squadron	Hurricanes	13	5	Pembrey

EXETER SECTOR

87 Squadron	Hurricanes	17	4	Exeter
601 Squadron	Hurricanes	14	6	Exeter

ST EVAL SECTOR

234 Squadron	Spitfires	16	1	St Eval
247 Squadron	Gladiators	9	-	Roborough

No 11 Group, HQ Uxbridge, Middlesex

KENLEY SECTOR

253 Squadron	Hurricanes	14	3	Kenley
501 Squadron	Hurricanes	18	1	Kenley
605 Squadron	Hurricanes	16	3	Croydon

BIGGIN HILL SECTOR

72 Squadron	Spitfires	10	7	Biggin Hill
92 Squadron	Spitfires	16	1	Biggin Hill
141 Squadron	Defiants	10	-	Biggin Hill
66 Squadron	Spitfires	14	2	Gravesend

NORTHOLT SECTOR

1 RCAF Squadron	Hurricanes	15	3	Northolt
229 Squadron	Hurricanes	19	-	Northolt
303 Polish Sqn	Hurricanes	15	4	Northolt
264 Squadron	Defiants	8	-	Northolt
504 Squadron	Hurricanes	15	-	Hendon

HORNCHURCH SECTOR

603 Squadron	Spitfires	14	5	Hornchurch
600 Squadron	Blenheims	13	5	Hornchurch
	Beaufighters	6	6	Hornchurch
41 Squadron	Spitfires	12	6	Rochford
222 Squadron	Spitfires	11	3	Rochford

NORTH WEALD SECTOR

249 Squadron	Hurricanes	17	1	North Weald
Half 23 Squadron	Blenheims	7	5	North Weald
	Beaufighters	5	-	North Weald
46 Squadron	Hurricanes	14	3	Stapleford Tawney

DEBDEN SECTOR

17 Squadron	Hurricanes	15	3	Debden
73 Squadron	Hurricanes	14	-	Castle Camps
257 Squadron	Hurricanes	14	4	Martlesham Heath
Half 25 Squadron	Blenheims	5	5	Martlesham Heath

TANGMERE SECTOR

213 Squadron	Hurricanes	13	6	Tangmere
607 Squadron	Hurricanes	19	1	Tangmere
602 Squadron	Spitfires	15	4	Westhampnett
Half 23 Squadron	Blenheims	10	5	Ford
	Beaufighters	1	-	Ford

No 12 Group, HQ Watnall, Nottinghamshire

DUXFORD SECTOR

242 Squadron	Hurricanes	17	-	Duxford
310 Czech Sqn	Hurricanes	18	2	Duxford
312 Czech Sqn	Hurricanes	4	5	Duxford
				Non operational
19 Squadron	Spitfires	14	-	Fowlmere

COLTISHALL SECTOR

74 Squadron	Spitfires	14	8	Coltishall

WITTERING SECTOR

1 Squadron	Hurricanes	16	2	Wittering
266 Squadron	Spitfires	14	5	Wittering

DIGBY SECTOR

611 Squadron	Spitfires	17	1	Digby
				To Fowlmere, morning 15th
151 Squadron	Hurricanes	17	1	Digby
29 Squadron	Blenheims	16	5	Digby
	Beaufighters	1	-	Digby

KIRTON IN LINDSEY SECTOR

616 Squadron	Spitfires	14	4	Kirton in Lindsey
264 Squadron	Defiants	6	4	Kirton in Lindsey
307 Polish Sqn	Defiants	8	8	Kirton in Lindsey forming

Junkers Ju 88

Ju 88 A-1, W.Nr. 3134, 9K+EL of KG 51. The KG 51 'Edelweiss' emblem is prominent on either side of the fuselage nose. This unit operated over the UK during the Battle.

Factory fresh Ju 88 As being given final checks on the factory flight line.

The Junkers Ju 88 was the most modern bomber in service with the *Luftwaffe* during the Battle, and it was stressed to carry out dive-bombing attacks. Its crew of four comprised: pilot, navigator/bomb-aimer, wireless-operator, rear gunner and flight engineer/ventral gunner. Normal cruising speed was 305 km/h (190 mph), with a maximum speed of 440 km/h (273 mph). If properly alerted and in a favourable position the Ju 88 could often use its speed in a dive to escape RAF fighters. Armament was up to four 7.9 mm machine guns in separate mountings and up to 1,000 kg (2,200 lbs) of bombs. The Junkers also served during the Battle in the photographic reconnaissance role.

Smoke rising from the fires
in the dockland area of
London on the afternoon
of 7 September, seen from
the roof of one of the
buildings overlooking
Fleet Street.

required more than thirty pumps, while a 'serious fire' required between eleven and thirty pumps to bring it under control.)

When the all-clear sounded on the morning of the 8th it was recorded that, in addition to the nine conflagrations, there had been nineteen major fires, forty serious fires and nearly a thousand smaller fires. Civilian casualties had been heavy: 430 killed and about 1,600 seriously injured.

London's fire brigades spent the daylight hours of the 8th in a desperate battle against the fires, well-knowing that any that remained would serve as beacons to guide bombers back to the capital that night. In spite of Herculean efforts, several fires resisted all attempts to extinguish them and there was light aplenty to guide in the two hundred bombers that returned to the city after darkness fell. The fires that had survived were fed afresh and several new ones were started. By the morning of the 9th, twelve conflagrations were raging. A further 412 people were killed and 747 seriously injured. The bombers would be back in force on the following night and, with one exception due to bad weather, on every one of the sixty-five nights that followed. The London great night *Blitz* had begun.

The huge blaze started at the Surrey docks on the night of 7/8 September continued to spread and it grew into the fiercest single fire ever recorded in Britain. It required 139 fire pumps to bring the conflagration under control.

'The long-awaited blow had fallen...'

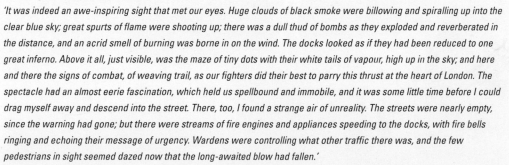

'It was indeed an awe-inspiring sight that met our eyes. Huge clouds of black smoke were billowing and spiralling up into the clear blue sky; great spurts of flame were shooting up; there was a dull thud of bombs as they exploded and reverberated in the distance, and an acrid smell of burning was borne in on the wind. The docks looked as if they had been reduced to one great inferno. Above it all, just visible, was the maze of tiny dots with their white tails of vapour, high up in the sky; and here and there the signs of combat, of weaving trail, as our fighters did their best to parry this thrust at the heart of London. The spectacle had an almost eerie fascination, which held us spellbound and immobile, and it was some little time before I could drag myself away and descend into the street. There, too, I found a strange air of unreality. The streets were nearly empty, since the warning had gone; but there were streams of fire engines and appliances speeding to the docks, with fire bells ringing and echoing their message of urgency. Wardens were controlling what other traffic there was, and the few pedestrians in sight seemed dazed now that the long-awaited blow had fallen.'

Wing Commander John Hodsoll, Inspector General of Air Raid Precautions, who watched the devastating 7 September attack on London's dock areas from the roof of the Home Office building in Whitehall.

During the second daylight attack on the city, on the afternoon of the 9th, cloud prevented accurate bombing. Twenty-five German aircraft were destroyed for a loss of eighteen British fighters. Two days later, on the 11th, the *Luftwaffe* mounted a daylight raid which added further damage to the dock areas. Fighter Command emerged from that action the loser – in shooting down twenty-four German machines, it lost twenty-eight Spitfires and Hurricanes. Three days later, on the 14th, German bombers attempted a further attack on the capital, only to be defeated yet again by cloud over the targets. On that day the *Luftwaffe* lost ten aircraft, Fighter Command lost twelve.

During the first four daylight attacks on London, for one reason or another, RAF fighter controllers had failed to bring a major proportion of their forces into action. On the initial attack, the shift against the capital had come as a surprise and the fighters had been positioned to block further attacks on airfields. During the next three attacks, the same banks of cloud that hindered accurate bombing had also prevented the tracking of the German formations by ground observers, making it difficult to vector RAF fighters into action. As we shall now observe, that unconnected series of failures would lead the *Luftwaffe* High Command to make an entirely erroneous assessment of the way the battle was progressing.

During the initial four daylight raids on London, *Luftwaffe* staff officers had noted that the bombers had not been engaged with the ferocity and effectiveness that had characterised many of the August actions. It seemed that Fighter Command might indeed be on the point of collapse, long predicted in the German calculations. (See page 45 'An Intelligence Trap Awaiting the *Luftwaffe*' in Chapter 2.) If RAF Fighter Command really was at its last gasp, the correct strategy would be to launch a series of large-scale attacks on the capital, to draw the

Although there was some collateral damage to residential areas during the daylight raids, it was the far-less-accurate night attacks that caused the most serious damage to civilian property and the heaviest civilian casualties. This bomb damage at Stepney Way, Stepney, was caused during the attack on the night of 7/8 September.

Messerschmitt Bf 110

A Messerschmitt Bf 110 C-5 of the reconnaissance unit, 4.(F)/Aufklärungsgruppe 4, which was forced down over England on 21 July 1940 by Hurricanes 238 Squadron. It was the first intact example of this type to be captured, and it was later re-painted in RAF markings in which it underwent flight testing.

The Messerschmitt Bf 110 C was the *Luftwaffe's* standard twin-engined fighter type during the Battle. Although its radius of action was sufficient to escort bombers to the more distant targets, the type was not manoeuvrable enough to dogfight successfully with RAF fighters. The aircraft carried a crew of two: pilot and wireless operator/rear gunner. The Bf 110 had a maximum speed of 562 km/h (349 mph) and carried an armament of two 20 mm cannon and four 7.9 mm machine guns firing forwards, and one 7.9 mm machine gun firing aft. During the Battle it served as a long-range escort fighter, fighter-bomber (carrying a bomb load of up to 1000 kg [2,200 lbs]), and also in the photographic reconnaissance role.

Future night fighter ace, Hans Joachim Jabs, stands before his Bf 110 of II./ZG 76 in the winter of early 1940.

Opposite page and right: The distinctive 'shark's mouth' marking on the noses of Bf 110s of ZG 76.

A sombre-looking Winston Churchill pictured with the Town Clerk of West Ham, Charles Cranfield, inspecting the gutted works of the Silvertown Rubber Company at Winchester Street on 8 September.

The attacks on London in September 1940 required the escorting Bf 109s to operate at close to the limit of their radius of action. As a result several were lost when they ran out of fuel on the way home. This example from JG 51 only just made it back to the coast of France.

remaining British fighters into action. They could then suffer further losses at the hands of the escorting Messerschmitts.

To that end, for 15 September the *Luftwaffe* planned to mount two separate daylight attacks on the British capital, with two hours between each. Every available Bf 109 unit in *Luftflotte* 2 was to support the attacks, with many escorts flying double sorties.

The first attack would be the conglomeration of rail lines at Latchmere junction, Battersea, a nodal point in London's rail system. The other strike would be yet another attack on four major dock areas: the Surrey Commercial Dock, the West India Dock, the Royal Victoria Dock and the Royal Albert Dock. Apart from the physical damage caused, these attacks would strike a further blow at civilian morale by demonstrating the vulnerability of the capital to attack.

Smoke plumes mark the funeral pyres of two Heinkels, one from KG 1 and the other from KG 26, which were shot down within a few hundred yards of each other near Lydd, in Kent, on 11 September.

This photograph was taken at Gravesend, in Kent, in late September 1940, and it shows a No 66 Squadron Spitfire coming in to land at the completion of a patrol. In the foreground is R6800, which was regularly flown by the unit's CO, Squadron Leader Rupert 'Lucky' Leigh. He had the fighter adorned with a rarely seen pre-war rank pennant below the cockpit, as well as a red propeller spinner. Parked behind R6800 is a Hurricane I of No 501 'County of Gloucester' Squadron, which also operated out of Gravesend at the time, despite technically being based at Kenley.

Lucky escape for Plt Off Alan Wright of No 92 Squadron. During a combat with Bf 109s on 9 September an enemy round fired from behind, passed through his Perspex canopy, bounced off the inside of the toughened glass windscreen and smashed his reflector gun sight. Wright was fortunate to escape without injury.

Warehouses burning at St Katherine's Dock, on the night of 11 September.

London Burning

In the book *Front Line*, the historian of the London Fire Brigade recorded:

'At Woolwich Arsenal men fought the flames among boxes of live ammunition and crates of nitro-glycerine, under a hail of bombs directed at London's No. 1 military target. But in the docks themselves strange things were going on. There were pepper fires, loading the surrounding air heavily with stinging particles, so that when the firemen took a deep breath it felt like burning fire itself. There were rum fires, with torrents of blazing liquid pouring from the warehouse doors and barrels exploding like bombs themselves. There was a paint fire, another cascade of white-hot flames, coating the pumps with varnish that could not be cleaned for weeks. A rubber fire gave forth black clouds of smoke so asphyxiating that it could only be fought from a distance, and was always threatening to choke the attackers. Sugar, it seems, burns well in liquid form as it floats on the water in dockyard basins. Tea makes a blaze that is 'sweet, sickly and very intense'. One man found it odd to be pouring cold water on hot tea leaves. A grain warehouse when burning produced great clouds of black flies that settled in banks upon the walls, whence the firemen washed them off with their jets. There were rats in their hundreds.'

The first of the day's attacks on London was planned to open shortly before noon. The raiding force comprised twenty-one Messerschmitt Bf 109 fighter-bombers of *Lehr Geschwader* 2 and twenty-seven Dornier Do 17s of *Kampfgeschwader* 76, escorted by about a hundred and eighty Bf 109s. The fighter-bombers were to carry out diversionary attacks on railway targets in the south-eastern quarter of the city, then the Dorniers were to bomb rail viaducts and lines running through Battersea.

Almost from the start, the operation went wrong for the *Luftwaffe*. As the Dorniers were climbing towards the Pas de Calais to link up with their fighter escort, they ran into a layer

Luftwaffe bombers began to adopt temporary black paint for night operations as early as September 1940. Here a mechanic uses a portable heater to help start the engines of a He 111.

A Heinkel He 111 in night camouflage being towed by a captured French light tank.

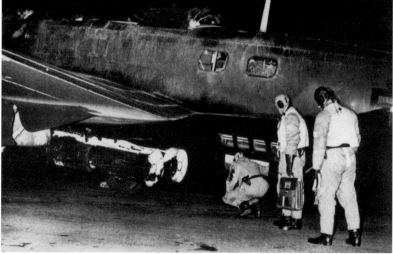

A crew from Kampfgeschwader 4 board a Heinkel He 111 for a night raid. The aircraft is loaded with two 1000 kg high explosive bombs on the external fuselage racks.

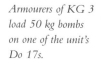

Armourers of KG 3 load 50 kg bombs on one of the unit's Do 17s.

Dornier 17s climbing to attack altitude in battle formation.

of cloud that was thicker than expected. The bombers were forced to break formation and their leader, *Major* Alois Lindemayr, had to orbit above cloud for several minutes to re-assemble his force. The bombers reached the Pas de Calais and picked up their escorts, then headed north-west for London. And again the weather took a hand in the proceedings, this time in the shape of a 144 km/h (90 mph) headwind at the bombers' altitude of 4880 metres (16,000 feet).

The small force of Bf 109 fighter-bombers was mistaken for an offensive fighter sweep by the *Luftwaffe*, and RAF pilots had orders to leave those alone if possible. As a result, these raiders reached the capital and delivered their attacks without interference from the defences. This was not a precision raid, however. The Messerschmitts scattered their bombs across the boroughs of Lambeth, Streatham, Dulwich and Penge, where they caused little damage and few casualties. They then withdrew without loss.

Meanwhile the Do 17s and their escorting Messerschmitts had to fight their way across the length of Kent, in a series of skirmishes involving eleven squadrons of Spitfires and Hurricanes. Due to the energetic cover provided by their escorts, the bombers reached the outskirts of London without a single loss and with their formation intact.

Now, however, the delays incurred in reforming the bomber formation over France, coupled with the need to battle against the powerful headwind, brought their inevitable outcome. When the raiding force neared the capital it was more than half an hour behind schedule. For the Dorniers that delay was not serious; they had plenty of fuel. But for the escorting Bf 109s it was another matter: even under optimum conditions London lay close to the limit of their effective radius of action. When they reached the eastern outskirts of the London they were low on fuel, and had to break away and head for home. By the time the Dorniers entered their bombing runs for the attack on Battersea, there were scarcely any escorts left.

Ignorant of his opponents' predicament, Air Vice Marshal Park had already decided to fight his main action over the eastern outskirts of London. To that end he ordered his fighter controllers to assemble twelve fresh squadrons to the east of the city. These squadrons flew in pairs, Spitfires with Spitfires and Hurricanes with Hurricanes. In addition, from Duxford near Cambridge, came a major reinforcement from No 12 Group: five squadrons of Squadron Leader Douglas Bader's 'Big Wing', going into action for the first time at its full strength of 35 Hurricanes and 20 Spitfires.

During their bombing runs the Dorniers held a tight formation, their gunners trading blows with their tormentors. But then one of the bombers suffered engine damage and was forced to leave the formation. The straggler immediately came under attack from several fighters, and was badly shot up. Three of the crew baled out; probably the other two were dead or too seriously wounded to join them.

The raiders released their bombs, then the formation entered a sweeping turn to port to begin their withdrawal. For its part the lone, straggling, pilotless Dornier continued doggedly heading north-west heading over the centre of the capital, still under attack from British fighters. Sergeant Ray Holmes of No 504 Squadron in a Hurricane ran in to attack the bomber from head-on, but shortly after he opened fire his Hurricane's guns fell silent – he was out of ammunition. Holmes later recalled: 'There was no time to weigh up the situation. His aeroplane looked so flimsy, I did not think of it as something solid and substantial . . . I thought my plane would cut right through it, not allowing for the fact that his plane was as strong as mine.' (Holmes was unaware the Dornier was by now effectively crewless).

A split second later the fighter's port wing struck the rear fuselage of the Dornier, shearing off the entire tail unit. Deprived of that vital appendage, the bomber's nose dropped violently. That imposed enormous forces on the outer wings, snapping them off out-board

A Dornier 17 releasing its load of twenty 50 kg bombs in a long stick.

of the engine nacelles as if they been made from balsa wood and tissue paper. The Hurricane had suffered severe structural damage also, and it too was falling out of control.

The Dornier entered a violent spin, still carrying its full complement of bombs. The savage G forces caused further failures of the aircraft's already-weakened structure and two 50 kg bombs and a container of incendiary bombs were wrenched off their mountings and smashed out the side of the bomb bay. One 50 kg bomb plunged into the roof of Buckingham Palace and passed through a couple of floors before it came to rest in the bathroom of one of the royal apartments. The other 50 kg bomb, and the container with sixteen incendiary bombs, landed in the Palace grounds. The fusing systems of the two larger bombs had not been made 'live', and neither weapon detonated. Some incendiary bombs ignited on hitting the ground, where they started small grass fires, but these were extinguished by members of the fire-watching team at the Palace.

Ray Holmes' Hurricane plummeted into the junction of Buckingham Palace Road and Pimlico Road, Chelsea. The fighter's engine, weighing about half a ton, smashed through the tarmac and rammed deep into the soil beneath, demolishing a water main in its path. The main part of the Dornier came down in the forecourt of Victoria Station, while the severed tail unit ended up on the roof of a house in Vauxhall Bridge Road.

Remarkably, considering that the bombs and the two wrecked aircraft fell on a built-up area, there were no injuries on the ground. Ray Holmes came down on the roof of a three-storey block of flats in Pimlico. Of the three German crewmen who baled out of the Dornier before it was rammed, two were taken into captivity soon after landing. The third man was less fortunate (See ... 'They went crazy' below).

As the formation of Dorniers began its homebound flight, it came under attack from more than twelve squadrons of fighters. One bomber, piloted by *Feldwebel* Rolf Heitsch, carried an infantry flame thrower intended for use against enemy fighters. One of Heitsch's engines was knocked out and he dived for the safety of a bank of cloud. Several fighters followed and as the first of these ran in to attack, the bomber's radio operator loosed off a burst

'They went crazy...'

'When the siren sounded, our bus came to a halt and I took cover in a doorway opposite The Oval underground station. Above us there were a lot of aircraft and a dogfight started, one of the bombers disintegrated in the air and three crewmen baled out. One of the crew came down beside the underground station. His parachute caught over electric power cables and he ended up dangling just above the ground. People came from all directions shouting "Kill him, kill him!" They pulled him down, they went crazy. Some women arrived carrying knives and pokers and they went straight in and attacked him. I felt sorry for the young lad, but there was nothing one could do. In the end an army truck arrived and the half-dozen soldiers had to fight their way through the crowd to get to him. They put him in the back of the truck and drove off..'

Walter Chesney, lorry driver, Streatham.
(Fatally wounded by the mob, the German airman died the following day.)

'They gave us tea and cakes...'

'The right motor of our Heinkel had been set on fire by the fighters' rounds. After we belly-landed the whole aircraft began to burn. I tossed into the flames my papers and my pistol so they would not fall into enemy hands. Then we scrambled out of the aircraft. Some soldiers arrived and started to shoot at us. We got down behind the burning aircraft and took cover. I took out my white handkerchief and waved it and the firing stopped. They approached us and I saw they were old men – Home Guard. After we were taken prisoner we were very well treated. It was a Sunday afternoon, the troops took us back to their barracks and gave us tea and cakes.'

Major Max Gruber, Heinkel He 111 navigator, *Kampfgeschwader* 53

On 15 September 1940, Sergeant Ray Holmes of No 504 Squadron rammed one of the Dorniers of KG 76 over London and the bomber crashed beside Victoria Station. Holmes baled out of his fighter and landed with minor injuries in Pimlico.

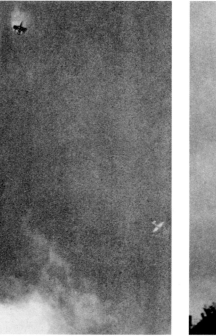

The port tail fin and rudder of the Dornier lies on a roof in Vauxhall Bridge Road.

Its tail unit (above right) and outer wing panels broken off, the Dornier Holmes had rammed spun out of the sky (above left). The wrecked Hurricane, minus its pilot, can be seen below it. Seconds after this photograph was taken, the Dornier crashed beside Victoria Station and the Hurricane crashed on the junction of Buckingham Palace Road and Pimlico Road, Chelsea.

Major Alois Lindmayr, the Kommandeur of III./KG 76, led the formation of Dorniers that raided London at noon on 15 September. Although shortage of fuel forced the escorting Messerschmitts to turn back for home short of the target, Lindmayr continued with the bombing run and his unit delivered an accurate attack. Then he conducted a brilliant fighting withdrawal in which three quarters of his force survived a ferocious and prolonged onslaught by twelve squadrons of Spitfires and Hurricanes.

of flame. On its first experimental test, the weapon proved worse than useless. In the rarefied air at high altitude, the oil fuel failed to burn properly and the weapon produced only a thin plume of flame about a hundred yards long. Moreover, far from scaring off any would-be attackers, the sight of the flame trailing behind the Dornier had exactly the opposite effect of that intended. To the RAF pilots it appeared that the Dornier was on the point of catching fire, and several fighters moved in for an easy kill. Heitsch's remaining engine was knocked out and he crash-landed the crippled bomber near Sevenoaks.

During the main action around the Dornier formation as it left the target area, nine other bombers suffered damage and were forced out of formation. Five of these were finished off in short order by RAF fighters. Then, near Maidstone, the Bf 109s assigned to cover the Dorniers' withdrawal linked up with their charges and shepherded them home. Assisting them was the same 90 mph wind that had impeded the raiders during their way in. Of the twenty-five bombers that crossed the coast of England, three-quarters of an hour earlier, six had been shot down and four were limping back to France. Most of the surviving Dorniers bore the scars of battle.

Kampfgeschwader 76 had taken a fearful mauling. Yet, considering the loss of the escorts over the target and the overwhelming concentration of RAF fighters engaging the formation, it is surprising that any Dornier survived. The fact that three-quarters of the bombers got home was testimony of the leadership of *Major* Alois Lindmayr, the commander of III./KG 76, and the discipline and flying skill of his crews. By reducing speed, he enabled damaged aircraft to remain within the protective firepower of the formation and thereby avoided a swift demise. By any yardstick, Lindmayr had conducted a remarkably successful fighting withdrawal.

As the noon raiders left the coast of England, the bombers assigned to the afternoon attack were airborne, assembled in formation and climbing towards the Pas de Calais. This raiding force was far larger than the previous one, with 114 Dorniers and Heinkels heading out to deliver yet another attack on London's battered dock areas.

Alerted by radar, the RAF fighter squadrons began scrambling shortly before 1400 hrs. As an initial move, eight squadrons were ordered to patrol in pairs over Sheerness, Chelmsford, Hornchurch and Kenley.

The vanguard of the *Luftwaffe* bomber force crossed the coast at Dungeness, the force wheeling on to a north-north-westerly heading. As it ran in over Kent, the formation comprised the three *Gruppen* of bombers in line abreast about three miles apart: on the left the Dornier Do 17s of *Kampfgeschwader* 2, in the centre the Heinkel 111s of *Kampfgeschwader* 53 and on the right the Dorniers of *Kampfgeschwader* 3 followed by the Heinkels of *Kampfgeschwader* 26. *Feldwebel* Heinz Kirsch of KG 3 described the mood in his Dornier as it crossed the coast: 'In our aircraft there was complete calm. The radio was silent. The safety

Unsuccessful secret weapon: an air test of the experimental flame thrower installation fitted to the Dornier flown by Feldwebel Rolf Heitsch of KG 76. When it was first used in action on 15 September, it attracted rather than discouraged enemy fighters, as RAF pilots saw it as an easy potential victim already on fire. The bomber came under repeated attack and it crash-landed near Sevenoaks. One crew member was fatally wounded, and Heitsch and the rest of the crew were taken prisoner.

catches were off, our steel helmets were on and each man searched his individual sector. Of the enemy there was nothing to be seen. In recent actions we had not had much contact with British fighters. We felt safe protected by the Bf 109s.'

Above Romney Marsh, the forward-deployed fighter squadrons went into action. The initial clash involved Nos 41, 92 and 222 Squadrons, with twenty-seven Spitfires, and these immediately became entangled with the escorting Messerschmitts.

As reports of the initial clash reached Park's headquarters his last two day-fighter units, Nos 303 and 602 Squadrons, were scrambled. All twenty-one of No 11 Group's Spitfire and Hurricane squadrons were now airborne and either in contact with the enemy or moving into position to engage. From No 12 Group, Squadron Leader Douglas Bader was again on his way south leading the five-squadron 'Big Wing'. And from the west No 10 Group sent a further three squadrons to protect the capital.

To defend London against this attack Fighter Command had amassed a total of two hundred and seventy-six Spitfires and Hurricanes, slightly more than during the noontime engagement. But the *Luftwaffe* raiding force was more than twice as large as the earlier one, and outnumbered the British fighters by more than two to one. In terms of fighters, there were three Bf 109s for every two Spitfires and Hurricanes.

The second wave of fighters to go into action comprised Nos 607 and 213 Squadrons, with twenty-three Hurricanes. They charged past the escorts and ran head-on into the Dorniers of *Kampfgeschwader* 3. Pilot Officer Paddy Stephenson of No 607 Squadron loosed off a short burst at one of the Dorniers and was about to pull his aircraft up to pass over his target, when another Hurricane moved in to block his escape route. Rather than collide with a friend, he decided to hold his course and rammed into one of the Dorniers. The Hurricane reared out of control, rolled on its back and went down in an inverted dive. Stephenson fought his way out of his cockpit, then clear of his stricken fighter. Meanwhile the shattered Dornier was also spinning out of control, and it plunged into a small wood near Kilndown in Kent with its crew still in the cockpit.

The battle around the bombers continued, as the Hurricanes split into sections and joined the Spitfires attempting to engage the bombers from astern and from the flanks. Again and again the Messerschmitts dived in to break up the attacks and drive off the RAF fighters. For their part the bomber crews held tight formation and mounted a powerful crossfire whenever a British fighter came within range.

For the Messerschmitt pilots assigned to the close escort, this was a particularly frustrating time. They were not permitted to pursue enemy fighters and go for a kill if that meant leaving their charges. Again and again the Messerschmitts had to break off the chase and return to their bombers, then the British fighters would return and the process had to be repeated.

Continued on page 101

A family pictured entering its Anderson Shelter. These steel structures were issued by the government for erection in back gardens, where they saved numerous lives.

Left and above: Bomb damage to rail lines in Battersea, inflicted during the attack on 15 September.

Further bomb damage to rail lines in Battersea, inflicted on 15 September.

Top and above: This badly shot up Dornier Do 17 of 4./KG 3 just made it back to its base in Belgium after the action on 15 September.

Everyone fighting in the air was both a potential victim and a potential killer

'As far as we were concerned the Battle was not a simple contest between single-engine fighter aircraft: it was a serious business of attacking all aircraft with black crosses as soon as contact was made. Our main job was to shoot down the bombers and avoid action with their fighters if we could. Over 11 Group the bombers' gunners shot down our Hurricanes and Spitfires and could be as dangerous as the Bf 109s. In Fighter Command more than 100 of our pilots were shot down and many others returned to base injured or [in aircraft] *shot up by the Luftwaffe bombers. The casualties included S/Ldr Peter Townsend; one seasoned Squadron Leader was shot down twice by enemy air gunners . . . Who were the victims in these actions? No one who had actually fought against German bombers could ever regard them as potential victims of no significance. Everyone fighting in the air was both a potential victim and a potential killer. Which one, or even both, they became was dependent on events and the casualties on both sides prove this.'*

Pilot Officer Peter Brown, Spitfire pilot, No 611 Squadron.

A rare joust between individual pilots

During the 15 September action there were numerous combats between opposing fighters, but few 'one-on-one' actions lasted more than 20 seconds. Anyone who concentrated his attention too long on one enemy fighter ran the risk of being blasted out of the sky by another. A rare exception of a longer combat took place that afternoon, however, when Squadron Leader Brian Lane, commander of No 19 Squadron, was attacked by a Bf 109. He pulled his Spitfire into a tight turn to avoid its fire, then moved in to deliver his riposte. As her recalled:

'He saw me as I turned after him and, putting on full inside rudder as he turned, skidded underneath me. Pulling round half stalled, I tore after him and got in a short burst as I closed on him before he was out of my sights again. That German pilot certainly knew how to handle a 109 - I have never seen one thrown about as that one was, and I felt certain that his wings would come off at any moment. However, they stayed on, and he continued to lead me a hell of a dance as I strove to get my sight on him again. Twice I managed to get in a short burst but I don't think I hit him, then he managed to get round towards my tail. Pulling hard round I started to gain on him and began to come round towards his tail. He was obviously turning as tightly as his kite could and I could see that his slots [on the leading edge of the wings] *were open, showing he was nearly stalled. His ailerons were obviously snatching too, as first one wing and then the other would dip violently.*

'Giving the Spitfire best, he suddenly flung out of the turn and rolled right over on his back passing across in front of me inverted. I couldn't quite see the point of this manoeuvre unless he hoped I would roll after him, when, knowing no doubt that my engine would cut [due to the float-type carburettor fitted to the Merlin engine] *whereas his was still going owing to the petrol injection system, he would draw away from me. Either that or he blacked out and didn't realise what was happening for a moment, for he flew on inverted for several seconds, giving me the chance to get in a good burst from the quarter. Half righting himself for a moment, he slowly dived down and disappeared into the clouds still upside down, looking very much out of control.*

'The sweat was pouring down my face and my oxygen mask was wet and sticky about my nose and mouth. I felt quite exhausted after the effort and my right arm ached from throwing the stick around the cockpit. At speed it needs quite a bit of exertion to move the stick quickly and coarsely in violent manoeuvres.'

Afterwards Lane claimed the enemy fighter 'probably destroyed' over Dartford. That claim links with no known German loss, however, and during the afternoon action on 15 September, no Bf 109 fell on land within 20 miles of Dartford.

As has been said, long manoeuvring combats between individual pilots were a rarity, since they required two pilots of above-average flying ability. More usually, successful fighter pilots engaging their enemy counterparts would follow the adage 'get in fast, hit hard, get out'.

Unteroffizer Figge brought this badly shot-up Dornier back to France, following the noon action on 15 September, and made a crash-landing near Poix. The bomber was damaged beyond repair, having collected more than two hundred hits from .303-in rounds.

Oberleutnant Florian, the aforementioned aircraft's observer wearing a field dressing to cover a wound, seen taking a swig from a bottle of wine brought by the rescue team. Above right: A close-up of the port wing of Figge's aircraft. On the original print more than fifty bullet hits can be counted, indicating that it had suffered attacks from one or more RAF fighters engaging from short range.

Return from London – 15 September 1940

'I returned to Antwerp on one engine. I did not land at my base, but at an emergency landing ground a little way away. I made a wheels-down landing on a meadow with both main wheels locked and the tyres cut to ribbons. As the Dornier touched down it stood on its nose, and slid along the ground on the nose and the two main wheels. When the aircraft came to a halt, the tail dropped to the ground with a crash. We were home!

'The radio operator lowered the entry hatch and a stream of spent cartridge cases dropped to the grass. Carefully we lowered the wounded flight engineer to the ground and carried him about 20 metres clear of the aircraft. Then we lit up cigarettes – that was one of the most enjoyable I ever smoked!

'At first there was nobody around, then some civilians appeared and finally some German soldiers arrived and summoned an ambulance. With the radio operator I walked round the aircraft to inspect the damage, stroking the trusty Dornier that had brought us home. There were more than two hundred bullet holes. I peeped inside the cowling of the starboard engine to see what was wrong with it. An entire cylinder head had been shot away and was lying in the bottom of the cowling.'

Feldwebel Horst Schulz, Dornier 17 pilot, *Kampfgeschwader* 3

Successful Luftwaffe Hoax

The Heinkel 100 D was built as a competitor to the Bf 109. But although it was faster, it was more difficult to handle and it was not ordered into production. In mid-1940, as a deliberate act of deception, nine of the twelve He 100 Ds built were painted in spurious unit markings and lined up for photographs intended to show the fighter, redesignated as the 'Heinkel 113', was in operational service. The hoax succeeded, and during the Battle, several RAF pilots reported engaging these aircraft and even shooting them down – though no wreckage was ever found to substantiate the claim.

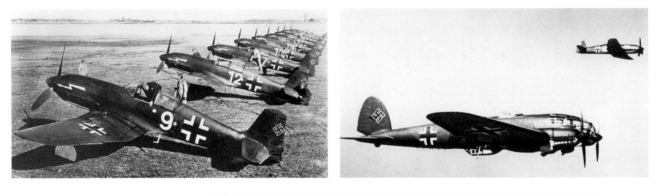

A bogus victory bar is painted on the tail of a 'Heinkel 113'. In fact this fighter never fired its guns in anger.

Next to join the mêlée were Nos 605 and 501 Squadrons, with fourteen Hurricanes. And now, four minutes after the loss of its first Dornier in a collision, *Kampfgeschwader* 3 lost another to the same cause. As Pilot Officer Tom Cooper-Slipper closed on one of the Dorniers, an accurate burst from the bomber slammed into the fighter and jammed its ailerons. Despite its pilot's frantic efforts, the Hurricane smashed into the bomber and both aircraft tumbled out of the sky. Cooper-Slipper baled out, as did the crew of the Dornier.

Feldwebel Horst Schultz, piloting one of the Dorniers, watched it happen: 'The British fighter came in from right to left, from the rear, and rammed into the Dornier. Then I saw three parachutes appear from the two aircraft as they went down. But again I could not spend much time watching, I had to hold formation or I would be joining them . . .'

Those in the bombers who observed the two collisions had no way of knowing that neither event was the result from a deliberate intention. To these watchers it seemed that the RAF was now in such desperate straits that its pilots had orders to ram the enemy bombers. If that was the case, the new tactic was proving devastatingly effective . . .

Following the initial attacks, the German escorts re-grouped and once again the action devolved into a series of short, fleeting, combats between the opposing fighters. The respite for the German bomber crews would be brief, however, for now they came within range of the anti-aircraft batteries deployed along the Thames. From the south and west of Chatham a concentration of twenty 4.5-in and eight 3.7-in guns opened up a heavy cannonade that caused damage to two bombers and forced them to leave the protection of their formations.

Now Fighter Command was at full stretch, with several squadrons in contact with the raiders and others converging on the enemy from all directions. On that day Winston Churchill chanced to be visiting Keith Park's underground operations room at Uxbridge, and he watched the action unfold on the plotting table:

'I became conscious of the anxiety of the Commander, who now stood still behind his subordinate's chair. Hitherto I had watched in silence. I now asked: "What other reserves have we?" "There are none," said Air Vice-Marshal Park. In an account which he wrote about it afterwards he said that at this I "looked grave". Well I might. What losses should we not suffer if our refuelling planes were caught on the ground by further raids of "40 plus" or "50 plus"! The odds were great; our margins small; the stakes infinite.'

At the time of the conversation, at about 1435 hrs on that fateful Sunday afternoon, every Spitfire and Hurricane squadron in No 11 Group and in the immediately adjacent sectors was airborne and committed to the action.

As during the action earlier that day, Park concentrated the bulk of his force immediately in front of London for the main engagement. No fewer than nineteen fresh squadrons were moving into position to the south and the east of the capital, with a total of one hundred and eighty-five Spitfires and Hurricanes.

Once again it was the Dorniers of *Kampfgeschwader* 3 that bore the brunt of the new attack. Heinz Kirsch remembered:

'A new call, "*Fighters dead astern!*" Something struck our machine. "*Hit on the left elevator!*" called the radio operator. Like a couple of shadows two Hurricanes swept over us, they came past so quickly we were unable to 'greet' them. More hits on our machine. And on top of that there was smoke in the cabin. The Tommies were staking everything they had; never before had we come under such heavy attack. After firing, the fighters pulled to the left or right to go past us. Some came so close I thought they were going to ram us.'

'I felt jolly glad to be down on the ground without having caught fire...'

Pilot Officer Eric Marrs flew Spitfires with No 152 Squadron. In a letter to his parents he described the action on 30 September 1940, when his fighter brought him home safely despite severe battle damage:

'We were just going in to attack when somebody yelled "Messerschmitts!" over the R/T and the whole squadron split up. Actually it was a false alarm. Anyway, being on my own I debated what to do. The bombers were my object so I snooped in under the 110s and attacked the bombers (about 40-50 Heinkels) from the starboard beam.

'I got in a burst of about three seconds when - Crash! – and the whole world seemed to be tumbling in on me. I pushed the stick forward hard, went into a vertical dive and held it until I was below cloud. I had a look round. The chief trouble was that petrol was gushing into the cockpit at the rate of gallons all over my feet, and there was a sort of lake of petrol in the bottom of the cockpit. My knee and leg were tingling all over, as if I had pushed them into a bed of nettles. There was a bullet hole in my windscreen where a bullet had come in and entered the dashboard, knocking away the starter button. Another bullet, I think an explosive one, had knocked away one of my petrol taps in front of the joystick, spattering my leg with little splinters and sending a chunk of something through the back of my petrol tank near the bottom. I had obviously run into some pretty good crossfire from the Heinkels.

'I made for home at top speed to get there before all my petrol ran out. I was about 15 miles from the aerodrome and it was a heartrending business with all that petrol gushing over my legs and the constant danger of fire. About five miles from the 'drome, smoke began to come from under my dashboard. I thought the whole thing might blow up at any minute, so I switched off my engine. The smoke stopped. I glided towards the 'drome and tried putting my wheels down. One came down and the other remained stuck up. I tried to get the leg that was down up again. It was stuck down. There was nothing for it but to make a one-wheel landing. I switched on my engine again to make the aerodrome. It took me some way and then began to smoke again, so I hastily switched off. I was now near enough and made a normal approach and held off. I made a good landing, touching down lightly. The unsupported wing slowly began to drop. I was able to hold it up for some time and then down came the wing tip on the ground. I began to slew round and counteracted as much as possible with the brake on the wheel which was down. I ended up going sideways on one wheel, a tail wheel and a wing tip. Luckily, the good tyre held out and the only damage to the aeroplane, apart from that done by the bullets, is a wing tip that is easily replaceable.

'I hopped out and went off to the M.O. to get a lot of metal splinters picked out of my leg and wrist. I felt jolly glad to be down on the ground without having caught fire.'

While Oxspring kept a wary eye on the enemy fighters, Leigh ordered the other Spitfires into line astern, entered a shallow dive to build up speed then pulled up steeply to attack the Heinkels from in front and below - the quarter where their defensive armament was weakest. Spitfire after Spitfire ran in to short range, fired a brief burst then broke away. High above, Bob Oxspring watched the Messerschmitts continue on their way unconcernedly. 'They did not seem about to interfere so I went down after the rest of the squadron and attacked one of the bombers from out of the sun. With .303-in ammunition you never knew if you had hit an enemy aircraft, unless you saw a flash or some obvious form of damage. The Heinkel broke away from the formation. I continued on, going down fast, and went through the formation.'

Next the Spitfires of No 72 Squadron attacked, followed by the Hurricanes of Nos 1 (Canadian) and 229 Squadrons. One of the bombers caught a lethal burst, it is not clear from whom, and fell out of the sky trailing smoke and flame. It smashed into open ground at Woolwich Arsenal. There were no survivors. Two other Heinkels, less seriously damaged, were forced to break formation and turn for home.

The escorting Messerschmitts, drawn from *Jagdgeschwader* 3, fought back resolutely to defend their charges and *Leutnant* Detlev Rohwer claimed the destruction of a Hurricane during this action. Probably his victim was Flying Officer Yuile of No 1 (Canadian) Squadron, who later recalled:

'We were diving in to attack a formation of Heinkels. I was so intent on watching the bombers that I forgot for a moment that we were supposed to have eyes in the side and back of our heads, as well as in front. A Messerschmitt that I had failed to notice flashed down on my tail and the next thing I knew something hit me in the shoulder with the force of a sledgehammer. An armour piercing bullet had penetrated the armour plate of the cockpit and got me. I was momentarily numbed, and when I swung round the German had gone.'

Yuile broke off the action and managed to bring his damaged fighter back to Northolt.

On the way to the target four German bombers had been knocked down, and seven had damage that forced them to leave formation and turn for home. All five formations of bombers reached London intact, however, and now they lined up to begin their bombing runs on their assigned targets in the dock areas.

During the day the cloud cover over southern England had built up appreciably, and now most of the capital lay beneath nine-tenths cumulus and strato-cumulus cloud with its base at about 2,000 feet and the tops extending to 12,000 feet. As luck would have it, every one of the bombers' briefed targets was now enshrouded in cloud. To the north of the Thames the only clear patch of sky lay over West Ham, and two formations of Heinkels and one of Dorniers re-aligned their runs and released their bombs on that borough. Throughout the area there was widespread damage.

Meanwhile the two formations of Dorniers of *Kampfgeschwader* 2, prevented by cloud from attacking the Surrey Commercial Docks to the south of the river, had turned through a semi-circle without bombing and now headed east. At that time three squadrons of Hurricanes had been battling with the escorts around this part of the raiding force, trying to force a way through. For these pilots the enemy U-turn was an unexpected delight, and convincing proof that by their very presence they had scared the Germans into turning back from attacking the capital. Afterwards several of them would say as much in their combat reports.

'The most serious and unpardonable error . . .'

'On 23 September our mission was a free-hunting sweep in the triangle Ramsgate-Canterbury-Folkestone, where British fighter activity had been reported. With three of my pilots I took off at 10.27 and headed towards Ramsgate in a slow climb to 4,500 metres [about 15,000 feet]. The weather was strange, with layers of cloud in which aircraft could easily hide. There were several flights of aircraft about which we saw for a moment before they disappeared, and we never knew if they were British or German. It was uncanny.

'We flew in wide curves, always changing altitude, never flying straight for long. We had been flying for 60 minutes, I thought that was enough and we were turning for home when I suddenly observed a Hurricane squadron between Ramsgate and Dover, twelve aircraft in four 'pulks'[1] flying one behind the other. They were about 1,000 metres below us and climbing in wide curves, like a creeping worm. My impression was that it was a Hurricane squadron on a training mission. The Hurricane pilots had no idea that four 109s were above them following each of their movements, like an eagle looking down on its prey.

'The spectacle was so fascinating that we completely forgot what was going on around us. That is the most serious and unpardonable error a fighter pilot can commit, and catastrophe immediately followed. Four Spitfires, of which we had been unaware due to our carelessness, attacked us from out of the sun. They fired at us from behind, roared close over our heads at high speed and disappeared back into the sky. As we broke formation fearing another attack from the Spitfires, I saw a 109 going down in flames on my right. It was Oberfeldwebel Knippsheer; we never found out what happened to him.'

Oberleutnant Hans Schmoller-Haldy, Bf 109 pilot, *Jagdgeschwader* 54.

[1] German aviators, slang for 'formation'.

Major Adolf Galland, seated second from left with pilots of Jagdgeschwader 26, beside his headquarters caravan at Caffiers near Calais.

Adolf Galland in his personal Messerschmitt Bf 109, in which he scored his thirty-third victory on 15 September.

Another view of Galland's Bf 109 E.

NIGHT BLITZ AND THE CIVILIANS' BATTLE CHAPTER 4

'I have night's dark cloak to hide me from their eyes.'

SHAKESPEARE: *ROMEO AND JULIET*

AT the beginning of October, having abandoned daylight attacks on Britain, the German bomber force confined itself almost entirely to night raids. And against these, as we have seen, the defenders had no effective counter. Unless bombers were held and illuminated by searchlights for half a minute or more, the anti-aircraft gun batteries had no means of locating the night raiders accurately enough to carry through an engagement. Even when they worked, the few available radar sets were little help. The Gunlaying Mark I radar had been designed to give only a general warning of approaching aircraft and range information. It did those things well enough, but the bearings it provided were generally inaccurate. Also, as there was no indication of elevation, the radar gave no height information. The set was, therefore, virtually useless for directing 'unseen' fire.

Had times been normal the gunners would have withheld their fire rather than waste expensive shells, but these were not normal times. There was strong political pressure on General Frederick Pile, the Commander of Anti-Aircraft Command, to present the sounds of an effective anti-aircraft defence even if the shells burst nowhere near the night raiders. The civilian population, ensconced in their shelters, would never know the difference. Accordingly Pile ordered his gunners to maintain a steady fire when night raiders were over the capital, even if there was no accurate fire control information. Later he wrote:

'The volume of fire which resulted, and which was publicised as a "barrage", was in fact largely wild and uncontrolled shooting. There were, however, two valuable results from it: the volume of fire had a deterrent effect upon at least some of the German aircrews . . . there was also a marked improvement in civilian morale.'

During that September the gunners loosed off about a quarter of a million anti-aircraft shells at night, most of them into thin air, and shot down less than twelve enemy aircraft.

At this time the RAF fighters operating at night were no more effective than the guns. The Blenheim, the main night fighter type, had the endurance to mount long patrols, and a few of them carried an early type of airborne interception (AI) radar. But the type had little margin of performance over the enemy bombers, so even if it found the latter it could rarely catch them. The single-seat Spitfires and Hurricanes sent to patrol at night had the performance to catch any raiders they found, but their endurance was short and since they lacked radar they could rarely find the enemy. The Defiants, all of which had been relegated to the night fighter role, had a short endurance and no radar. Yet for this role the turret fighter did have some useful attributes. Its two-man crew meant that it had two 'pairs of eyes' to search for the enemy bombers, and it had the performance to catch any that it found. Moreover, the gun turret enabled it to carry out surprise attacks from below and one side of the target, making it the most effective night fighter available in any numbers.

The Bristol Beaufighter, later fitted with AI (airborne interception) Mark IV radar, was the first really effective night fighter type to enter service with the RAF. It became available in useful numbers towards the end of 1940. Its maximum speed was 312 mph and it carried an armament of four 20 mm cannon and six .303-in machine guns.

The twin-engine Bristol Beaufighter seemed to provide an effective answer to the night bomber, but it had just entered production. It was heavily armed, with four 20 mm cannon and six .303-in machine guns, and had a good endurance. It had an excellent performance and some of these aircraft carried the latest type of airborne interception (AI) radar, the Mark IV. The new fighter was being pushed into service as rapidly as possible, but it suffered from teething troubles. A few months would elapse before it was operational in sufficient numbers to pose a serious threat to the night raiders.

During their night attacks on Britain, German bomber crews were often guided to targets by *Knickebein* radio beams radiating from powerful ground transmitters situated in France, Holland, Norway and Germany itself. The device proved a useful adjunct to night bombing. Flying along a beam aligned on his target, a bomber pilot heard Morse dots if he was to the left of the beam, Morse dashes if he was to the right of the beam, and a steady note if he was in the centre of the beam. A second *Knickebein* beam crossed the first at the bomb release point, allowing the bombs to be released with reasonable accuracy even if the crew could not see the target.

By the end of August 1940, the *Luftwaffe* had twelve *Knickebein* transmitters positioned to align their beams on targets in Britain. But also by then, Royal Air Force Intelligence had learned about the existence of the system. A specialised jamming unit, No 80 Wing, was formed to radiate jamming signals on the German beam frequencies. During the heavy night raids on Britain in September and October 1940, No 80 Wing's jamming caused many a German bomber to miss its target. Given the relative ineffectiveness of the other systems dealing with the night bombers, No 80 Wing quickly became a significant addition to the nation's air defences.

Throughout October 1940, apart from a few nuisance raids by individual twin-engined bombers, the great majority of the daylight attacks on Britain were carried out by bomb-carrying Messerschmitt Bf 109s and Bf 110s. The fighter-bombers carried small bomb loads

A 'Knickebein' beam transmitter at Stollberg in Schleswig Holstein – one of those used to guide night bombers to targets in Britain. The huge aerial array was about 30.5 metres (100 feet) high, and it was rotated on to the bearing of the target by means of railway bogies running on a track 96 metres (315 feet) in diameter. The Knickebein beam in fact comprised two overlapping beams, with Morse dots radiated in one and Morse dashes in the other. Where the beams overlapped the dots and the dashes interlocked to produce a steady note. The bomber crew flew along the steady note lane from one transmitter, and released their bombs as they passed through the steady note lane from a second transmitter which crossed the first at the bomb release point. Using transmitters situated in France, Holland and Norway, the Luftwaffe could align two or more beams over any target in Great Britain. Using this system raiders could release their bombs with sufficient accuracy to hit a large area such as a city, without the crew needing to see their target.

– a maximum of 250 kg (550 lbs) for a Messerschmitt 109 and 1000 kg (2,200 lbs) for a Bf 110. During their attacks on London and other large targets, the fighter-bombers released their bombs from around 4876 metres (16,000 feet). Since these aircraft were not fitted with proper bombsights, their bombing accuracy was poor. Compared with the concentrated damage caused previously by twin-engined bombers attacking by day, or the widespread destruction being caused by the night bombers, the damage inflicted by the fighter-bombers was insignificant.

Politically it was unacceptable to allow enemy aircraft to deliver attacks on London at will, and Fighter Command was forced to make every effort to engage these fleeting targets. Yet the fighter-bomber raids presented an extremely difficult interception problem. In a high speed dash at altitudes around 7620 metres (25,000 feet) or above, the bomb-carrying Messerschmitts could reach the outskirts of the capital within 17 minutes of the defenders receiving the first radar warning of their approach. Yet from the order to scramble, a squadron of Spitfires required about 22 minutes to reach 25,000 feet (a squadron of Hurricanes required about three minutes longer). Thus Fighter Command's normal scramble tactic, of taking off once the radar warning had been received, was no longer viable; had that method been used, the RAF fighters would have reached the capital between five and eight minutes after the raiders had completed their attack. If the enemy raiders were to be intercepted before they

These colour photographs show predominantly Bf 109 E-1 Jabos ('Jagdbomber' – fighter-bombers) of JG 53. Throughout September and October, JG 53 was very active in the Jabo role – two or more sorties per day being the rule rather then the exception, and rest days were taken only when bad weather prevented flying.

The cockpit of a Bf 109 Jabo (fighter-bomber), showing the bomb selection panel at centre lower (between the rudder pedals).

Ground crew running engine checks on a Dornier Do 17 Z of 9./KG 76.

Ground crew at work on a He 111 of I./KG 26.

Ground crewmen turn the crank handle for the inertia starter of a Junkers Ju 88, with four 250 kg (550 lb) bombs on the underwing racks, ready for a night mission.

reached London, the defending fighters would need to be already airborne at 10,000 feet or above, when the first radar plots were received on the incoming fighter-bombers.

To counter the new threat, No 11 Group was forced to mount standing patrols over south-eastern England throughout the day. It meant a lot of flying, and general wear and tear on the Spitfires and Hurricanes for relatively little action, but there was no alternative. Fighters were sent off in relays to cruise on set patrol lines at 15,000 feet, the highest altitude at which they could operate without their pilots needing to use the fighters' limited supply of oxygen. When an incoming raiding force was detected on radar, the fighters climbed to altitude and were vectored into position to engage the intruders.

Representative of the actions during this period were those fought between dawn on 15 October and dawn on the 16th. Early on the 15th, two separate formations of Messerschmitts reached London and dropped their bombs over a large area. The only significant damage was to Waterloo main line station, which was hit by a bomb that halted services for several hours until repairs could be completed. Also during the day German fighters flew sweeps over southern England. In a series of scrappy actions seven Bf 109 fighters and fighter-bombers were shot down, but the RAF lost twelve aircraft. Technically the attackers had won that day's contest 'on points', but such nuisance raids would never produce a decisive result.

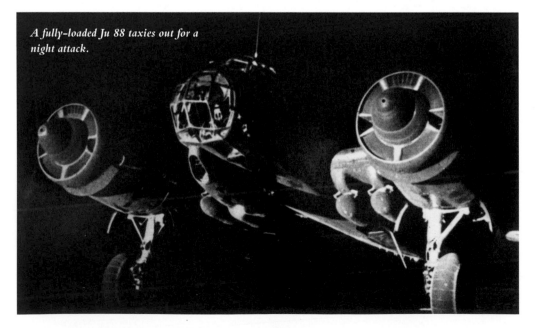

A fully-loaded Ju 88 taxies out for a night attack.

After dark on the 15th, the *Luftwaffe* delivered yet another heavy attack on London, commencing at 2040 hrs and continuing through to 0440 hrs the following morning. It was a bright moonlight night and the raiding force of some four hundred bombers, drawn from *Luftflotte* 2, approached the city from several directions at altitudes above 16,000 feet. Bomber crews reported encountering barrage fire over the capital, with shells detonating at altitudes between 13,000 and 20,000 feet, strongest over the eastern and southern sectors.

One pilot who took part in the attack was Günther Unger of *Kampfgeschwader* 76, recently promoted to *Feldwebel*. His crew was one of several that flew two sorties that night, one on the evening of the 15th and another during the morning darkness on the 16th. On both occasions his target was one of the dock areas, and his orders were to remain over the target for as long as possible to cause maximum disruption to those on the ground. To that end he was briefed to circle over the target and release a single bomb every five minutes or so. Displaying a realistic contempt for the so called 'London barrage', Unger spent about twenty-five minutes circling over the target on each sortie.

Forty-one Royal Air Force fighters took off to engage the raiders that night, but there were only two interceptions. One was by a Blenheim of No 23 Squadron, whose radar operator made contact with one of the enemy bombers. The aircraft's poor performance prevented it getting into a firing position, however, and after a lengthy tail-chase the raider escaped.

The other interception, by Pilot Officer Hughes and Sergeant Gash in a Defiant of No 264 Squadron, resulted in the destruction of a He 111 of *Kampfgruppe* 126. That engagement, the defenders' only success that night, is described in 'Defiant Victory' on the following page.

A battery of 3.7-in anti-aircraft guns in Hyde Park firing a salvo. Despite the wartime propaganda on the effectiveness of the London gun defences, their uncontrolled shooting caused little damage to enemy aircraft and did not cause undue worry to their crews. The guns were, however, successful in one important aspect: by forcing raiders to attack from 10,000 feet and above at night, there was a consequent reduction in bombing accuracy. Also, for those residing in the capital and in their shelters, the noise of the guns firing and shells exploding provided the shadow, if not the substance, of an effective air defence.

A Boulton Defiant of No 264 Squadron taxies out for a night interception patrol.

Defiant victory

'It was a bright moonlight night. Suddenly, out of the corner of my eye, I saw something move across the stars out to my left. If you are scanning the night sky it is normally completely still, so anything that moves attracts the eye. This just had to be another aircraft. I got Fred [Sergeant Fred Gash, the Defiant's gunner] to swing his turret round and we both kept an eye on the black shape. We moved towards it and soon caught sight of the row of exhausts. It was a twin-engined aircraft. I slid alongside, below and to the right of him, and slowly edged in "under his armpit" while Fred kept his guns trained on the aircraft. Then we saw the distinctive wing and tail shape of a Heinkel – there was no mistaking it. I moved into a firing position, within about 50 yards of his wing tip and slightly below, so that Fred could align his guns for an upwards shot at about 20 degrees. Obviously the German crew had not seen us, for they continued straight ahead. Fred fired straight into the starboard engine. One round in six was a tracer, but what told us we were hitting the Heinkel was the glitter of the de Wilde [incendiary] rounds as they ignited on impact. Fred fired, realigned, fired again. He got off two or three bursts. There was no return fire from the bomber – indeed, I doubt if any guns could have been brought to bear on our position on its beam. The engine burst into flames, then the Heinkel rolled on its back, went down steeply and crashed into a field near Brentwood. We heard later that two of the crew had baled out and were taken prisoner.'

Pilot Officer Desmond Hughes, Defiant pilot, No 264 Squadron.

That night London's rail system was hit particularly hard. The termini at St Pancras, Marylebone, Broad Street, Waterloo and Victoria were put out of action for varying periods. Further damage reduced traffic into and out of Euston, Cannon Street, Charing Cross and London Bridge stations. A chance hit blew a hole in the Fleet Street sewer, and the escaping waters flooded the rail tunnel between Farringdon Street and King's Cross stations. Beckton gas works, Battersea Power Station and the BBC headquarters at Portland Place were hit, three large water mains were fractured and there was widespread damage in residential areas. More than 900 fires were reported in the capital, six of which were 'major' and nine 'serious'.

Although London was the bombers' main target, it was not the only one. Twenty He 111s of *Kampfgruppe* 100 attacked Birmingham and eight Dorniers of *Kampfgruppe* 606 raided Bristol. Elsewhere bombs fell on Southend, Windsor, Portsmouth, Yeovil, Southampton, Bournemouth, Plymouth, Tunbridge Wells, Hastings, Reigate and Eastbourne.

Continued on page 122

Bomb damage at Tottenham Court Road on the morning of 25 September, after the raid on the previous night.

On the evening of 14 October, a bomb fell in Balham High Road about 100 yards from the underground station, and blew a large crater. The bomb exploded about 25 yards in front of the moving bus (seen here) and driver George Hitchen had a narrow escape; he was blown from his cab and ended up in a shop doorway with cuts and bruises. Others were less fortunate. Sixty-eight people were killed in the incident, many of whom had been taking shelter in the station. The explosion took off the top of the Northern Line tunnel and caused severe flooding. It was more than three months before the damage could be repaired and the line reopened.

Bomb damage in Leicester Square on the morning of 17 October, in front of the headquarters of the Automobile Association. The damage to the vehicles in the foreground was too bad, even for that organisation's esteemed experts to repair!

Blitz on Britain

The docklands burn.

A fire weakened building collapses.

Rescue workers take a tea break.

Rescuing a trapped and injured Londoner.

London burns.

'London can take it': firemen at work.

Hoisting a barrage balloon over the Tower of London.

Life goes on: a typical London street scene following a German bombing raid.

Hell on Earth – 1

Notting Hill, London

'One evening after the sirens had sounded their usual warning and nothing much happened, there was a sound like stones being thrown against the house or a number of slates falling off the roof. We ran to the front door and found an incendiary bomb burning brightly on the mat. Roland dashed upstairs for the bucket of sand he kept for just such an emergency; I ran into the kitchen and snatched up a bowl of washing-up water. The suds doused the bomb, snuffing it like a candle.

'From the doorway we could see that there were many other incendiaries, some burned out harmlessly in the road or basement area, some on houses and one on the back seat of a car, having burned though the roof. Roland dumped his bucket of sand on that one and was pleased that it obediently went out. The bombs were about nine inches long and burned with a white light for three or four minutes, leaving only their tail fins.

'The daughter of a trapped woman was standing on her doorstop crying hysterically. Roland asked her which room her mother was in. "Second floor. But she's dead, oh poor mum, she's dead. I know she's dead."

'Roland gave me a full bucket of water and kept the stirrup pump himself. We soaked handkerchiefs, tied them over our nose and mouth and went up the smoke-filled stairs on our hands and knees. He kicked open the bedroom door. The room was full of smoke but there was a red glow in one corner and he crawled towards this. I pumped and he directed the spray. The incendiary had crashed through the roof and the bedroom ceiling, landing on the bed. All the smoke in the house was coming from the burning mattress and bedding. The bomb had long since burned itself out and the spray soon had the fire out. As the smoke cleared we could see an old lady in the bed. She was quite dead.

'Once outside again we were grabbed by a little old man in a white muffler, who begged us to put out some incendiaries lodged in his attic. We got those out fairly quickly but then he pointed to a ladder and an open sky light, saying that there were more on the roof. Somehow I found myself edging along the peak of the roof clutching a stirrup pump, while Roland came behind with a bucket.

The view across the ruined streets of London as seen from St Paul's Cathedral.

Workers fill in a bomb crater in the road outside Buckingham Palace.

'From up there we could see down into the street and way over the rooftops. It was an extraordinary sight: all around the horizon fires glowed, searchlights raked the dark sky, anti-aircraft guns flashed silently, there being no apparent connection between them and the almost continuous noise of the guns. High above us, shells burst like fireworks. But the most insistent noise came from the street immediately beneath us. It was the excited sound of many people shouting as they scurried in and out of their houses.

'I started to spray the incendiary lodged by the chimney when I heard the sound of more bombs coming down and hugged the peak of the roof. Moments later a stick of small, 50-pound, high explosive bombs fell in a line across houses and street.

'The bombers, earlier in the evening, had dropped nothing but hundreds of incendiaries. But this wave, a couple of hours later, came back with instantaneous high explosive bombs where the fires were brightest and most people were in the streets.

'The explosions caused panic. People ran back into burning houses or threw themselves into the basement area. I heard screams above the explosions, as I tried to dig myself into the slates of the roof.

'The rain of bombs lasted only a few minutes but it was dawn before the fires were all out and the injured had been taken away. We sat in the kitchen of our house drinking cocoa with neighbours who had lived near each other for years but had never spoken. Now they were talking and gesticulating in a most un-English manner as they described the narrow escapes of the night.'

Peter Elstob, London resident

Hell on Earth – 2

'They said there was a risk from incendiary bombs and the safest place to sleep was on the ground floor. So we moved two single beds down for my two eldest sons. I slept upstairs on my own, as my husband was away on duty with the ARP heavy rescue team. We had all gone to bed, the four youngest children in the shelter in the garden.

'This oil bomb hit the house at about 3 o'clock in the morning. I never heard a thing. Then a high explosive bomb landed nearby and that woke me up, it threw me out of bed and on to the landing. When I got downstairs the whole room was on fire. There was dreadful black oil all over the place, burning. My 18-year old son was trapped in his bed. He couldn't move, his legs must have been damaged when the bomb came through the ceiling. He was alight from head to foot, sitting up in bed. My other son who was sleeping in the room, my next-door neighbour and I tried to pull him away from the bed, but his skin came away in our hands. He didn't scream or anything, he was just shaking his head from side to side. All he said to me was "Save yourself!" We threw a bucket of water over him, but water was no good against oil. So we threw a bucket of sand over him and that put out some of the flames.

'Then an ambulance came and they carted us away to hospital. I was moaning the whole time and I heard the nurse say "Admit her, Admit her!" I had broken my ankle and my arms and hands were burned. I was wearing a nightdress and a coat, they had to cut them off me. I was so ill with shock that I had several blankets and a couple hot water bottles and I was still shivering.

'I never saw my eldest son again. He died the next morning, they said from shock. I was in hospital for a week then I discharged myself. My 16-year-old son was also burned, he was in hospital for three weeks, then he came out on crutches. The children in the shelter were all right. I wanted to go home but I had no home. The house was burned down and I had lost all my furniture. So we went to my brother-in-law's.

'Ever since then I have been terrified of fire. It just creeps up on you, you don't hear anything.'

Mrs E.M., resident of Carshalton

The day and night actions over Britain continued in this vein throughout October, punctuated by periods of autumnal bad weather that restricted air activity on twelve days during that month.

On the night of 25 October there was a new departure: making its first appearance over Britain, the newly arrived Italian Air Force contingent launched sixteen Fiat Br 20 bombers to attack Harwich from its base in Belgium. The changeable weather conditions over northern Europe presented the newcomers with unforeseen problems, however. One bomber crashed on take-off, and two more ran short of fuel on their return flights and their crews were forced to bale out. Little damage was caused at the port.

Four days later the Italian force was over England again, this time by day. On the 29th, a force of fifteen Fiat Br 20s, escorted by seventy-three CR 42 biplane fighters attacked Ramsgate. The raiders were not intercepted by defending fighters, but several bombers suffered damage from anti-aircraft fire and the raid caused little damage on the ground.

According to official British accounts, the daylight part of the Battle of Britain ended on 31 October 1940. Yet the fighting continued, although with diminishing intensity, well into November.

If any action can be said to characterise this running down phase of the Battle, it is that of the morning of 1 November. Shortly after daybreak, at 0735 hrs, Hurricanes of Nos 253 and 605 Squadrons took off to mount a standing patrol in the Maidstone area; soon afterwards Spitfires of Nos 41 and 603 Squadrons left the ground for a similar patrol over Rochford. Just before 0800 hrs an incoming enemy force was observed on radar leaving the coast of France near Boulogne. The strength of the hostile force was assessed a '9 plus' but no height information was available (that usually meant the raiders were either above, or below, the altitude measuring capability of the Chain Home radar stations).

For all the hardship, a smile can still be raised.

The fate of some of those bombed out of their homes

'I slept the night in the cinema. It is lit by six large lights, four of these are turned off at eleven o'clock, the other two remain on all night. Firemen and nurses patrol the cinema throughout the night, the nurses tucking up children, fetching water and milk and so on. Each family takes a small piece of ground as their own province. Some are in the orchestra pit, and are given a little privacy by the curtains in front of it. But the majority sleep in the gangways and between the seats . . .

'All are provided with blankets and palliasses. These they park somewhere and put their belongings (mostly a change of clothing) on the seats nearby. When it is bed time the men take off their coats, the women their overalls, and lie down. The gangways become crowded, people lying very close to one another. Between the seats there is perhaps an average of one person to a row of ten seats. Here and there is a baby in his pram. There is no noise during the night, except for babies crying. Nearly every mother has a small child, and as soon as one cries, three or four others start too. It quite impossible to get more than ten minutes' uninterrupted sleep.'

Extract from Mass Observation Survey

At 0805 hrs about ten high-flying Bf 109 fighter-bombers, with fighter escort, crossed the coast near Dover. The raiders penetrated to the Sittingbourne area, dropped their bombs and made off before they could be intercepted.

Fifteen minutes later a similar formation of fighter-bombers, with escorts, crossed the coast heading for Canterbury. Eleven Hurricanes of No 605 Squadron intercepted the Messerschmitts near Faversham and a sharp combat developed. The sole loss on either side was the Hurricane squadron commander Squadron Leader Archie McKellar, who was killed.

For a while there was a period of calm, and fresh squadrons took off to relieve those on the patrol lines. At 1015 hrs four Spitfires of No 92 Squadron were directed to intercept a single high flying intruder over Kent. Five minutes later the defenders sighted the enemy

The fate of many children in London was evacuation to parts of the country considered safe from the Luftwaffe.

machine at 29,000 feet near Dover, a Messerschmitt Bf 110 on reconnaissance. Two Spitfires reached firing positions and their pilots reported hits, and when last seen the aircraft was heading out to sea streaming glycol from its damaged cooling system. The Messerschmitt crash-landed near Calais with both crewmen wounded.

At 1100 hrs Hurricanes of Nos 229 and 615 Squadrons were on patrol over Maidstone when the next raiding force, about thirty-five Bf 109s in two formations, crossed the coast near Dover. Hurricanes of Nos 253 and 501 Squadrons were immediately scrambled to reinforce the defence, and all four squadrons were vectored toward the raiders. No Hurricane made contact with the enemy, however.

Half an hour later Spitfires of Nos 74 and 92 Squadrons, then on the Maidstone patrol line, had a brush with Messerschmitts but there was no loss on either side.

So ended the actions on the morning of 1 November. For the pilots of Fighter Command this was a frustrating time, with much time spent waiting on the patrol lines or at readiness on the ground, but few chances to engage the enemy.

During the period between 1 October and 1 November, the *Luftwaffe* lost 297 aircraft while the Royal Air Force lost 152 fighters. That meant a ratio of 1.9:1 in favour of the defenders, higher than during the previous phase though set against a background of far less intensive fighting.

Just as the Battle of Britain had begun with a gradual build-up over several weeks in July and the early part of August, so the pattern of daylight actions over southern England ran down gradually during October and November. The night raids on Britain's cities would continue with undiminished fervour throughout the winter and into the spring 1941, ending with a crescendo in May before the main part of the *Luftwaffe* bomber force moved to bases in eastern Germany and Poland in preparation for the attack on the Soviet Union. Only after Hitler had committed his war machine to that all-consuming adventure, would the British people gain a lasting respite from the devastating attacks on their cities.

Fire hoses lie like giant spaghetti the morning after a raid, testimony to the furious battle with the fires.

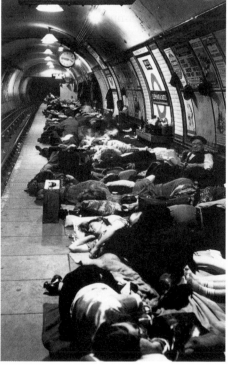

The London Underground became a crude but essential and largely effective means of sheltering civilians from the daily onslaught of the Luftwaffe.

Upper right: Defiance.
Right: Firemen survey damage and begin to clean-up in the City of London.

A night raider remembers

'I have no particular memories of individual night operations. They were all quite routine, like running a bus service. The London Flak defences put on a great show – at night, the exploding shells gave the place the appearance of bubbling pea soup. But very few of our aircraft were hit – I myself never picked up so much as a shell fragment. On rare occasions one of my crew might catch sight of a British night fighter, but it seems they never saw us and we were never attacked. During our return flights the radio-operator would often tune in his receiver to a music programme, to provide some relief from the monotony.'

London burns - as viewed by a Luftwaffe air crew.

Unteroffizier Horst Götz, Heinkel He 111 pilot, *Kampfgruppe* 100.

A night fighter pilot remembers

'It might seem a simple matter for night fighter crews to see the bombers which had been illuminated by searchlights, but this was not the case. If the raiders came on bright moonlit nights, which was usual during this time, the beams of the searchlights were not visible at heights much above 10,000 feet. If the searchlights were actually on the enemy bomber, the latter could be seen from some way away, but only if the fighter was beneath the bomber and could see its illuminated underside; if the fighter was higher than the bomber, the latter remained invisible to the fighter pilot. If there was any haze or cloud it tended to diffuse the beams so that there was no clear intersection to be seen, even if two or more searchlights were accurately following the target.'

Pilot Officer Dick Haine, Blenheim night fighter, No. 600 Squadron.

Sgt. Alan Stuart Harker, No. 234 Squadron

Despite claiming eight victories during the Summer of 1940, one of the lesser-known RAF pilots who flew during the Battle of Britain was Sgt. Alan Stuart Harker of 234 Squadron. Born on 16 July 1916 in Bolton, Lancashire, Alan Harker began pilot training when he joined the RAFVR in October 1937. His first solo flight– in a De Havilland Tiger Moth on 12 March 1938 – lasted all of five minutes, Harker afterwards writing in his logbook, '*Whew, what a relief to be down in one piece.*'

On 1 September 1939, Harker was officially called up for service, and on the 12th he was posted to 10 FTS at Ternhill, Shropshire, flying Avro Ansons. When his training was completed, he was posted on 5 November 1939 to the newly reformed 234 Squadron at Leconfield, near the Humber, a fighter squadron originally intended for shipping protection duties which operated a mixture of Blenheims, Battles and Gauntlets. Harker flew the squadron's Bristol Blenheims, but in March 1940, 234 Squadron began to receive Spitfires and became operational on them in May.

On 10 August, Harker landed at St. Eval, Cornwall, with the undercarriage of his aircraft still retracted. Although he could hear the control tower shouting at him over the radio to lower his wheels, he was so exhausted that he was unable to respond. Nevertheless, he was summarily reprimanded by the squadron CO for carelessness which resulted in Category 2 damage to Spitfire P9468.

On 14 August, 234 Squadron moved to the airfield at Middle Wallop and into the thick of the action, the airfield being bombed all afternoon by He 111s and Ju 88s. The next day the squadron, together with the Hurricanes of 43 Squadron, was ordered off to intercept a raid on Portland being conducted by Ju 87s escorted by Bf 110s and 60 Bf 109s. While 43 Squadron attacked the Bf 110s and Ju 87s, 234 Squadron attacked the Bf 109s, but a single squadron could do little against the Messerschmitts and it was overwhelmed by numbers. Three of the squadron's Spitfires were lost and Sgt. Harker considered himself fortunate to escape with his life. This experience was obviously taken as a salutary warning, for on the 16th, when Harker was chased by three yellow-nosed Bf 109s, he obviously decided that discretion was the better part of valour and, determined to be more careful, took refuge in cloud. One interesting aspect of the fighting on the 15th and 16th was that the squadron received false R/T messages from the Germans ordering it to 'Pancake' (land immediately).

Sgt. Harker's first victory came on 18 August when Ju 87s attacked the airfields at Gosport, Ford and Thorney Island. While three other RAF squadrons attacked the dive-bombers, 234 Squadron engaged the Bf 109 fighter escort provided by I. and II./JG 27. In the air battle which ensued, no fewer than 16 Ju 87s were shot down and of the six Bf 109s which JG 27 lost that day, two were claimed by Sgt. Harker and witnessed by P/O Gordon.

On 4 September, 234 Squadron was patrolling near Tangmere when it was ordered eastwards where it encountered the Bf 110s of III./ZG 76. In the running battle which followed, several pilots from 234 Sqn. claimed to have destroyed Bf 110s,

Sgt. Alan Harker seated in Spitfire AZ-N of 234 Squadron, probably at St. Eval in Cornwall in August/September 1940.

This photograph, believed taken in October 1940, shows the original aircraft name has been painted out, and replaced by 'NELLORE', a city in south-east India which had raised a financial contribution towards the cost of the machine. At about the time of this photograph, Sgt. Harker was awarded the DFM in recognition of his achievements in the Battle of Britain when, as may be seen from the row of Swastikas under the windscreen, he claimed eight enemy aircraft destroyed. He was commissioned in May 1940.

Sgt. Harker claiming one which he saw crash near Brighton. His logbook for the day contains an entry stating that the squadron shot down all 15 aircraft in a German defensive circle, but while it is true that the *Luftwaffe* lost no fewer than 17 Bf 110s on this day, only six were from III./ZG 76 - the *Gruppe* attacked by 234 Sqn. – and there were also a number of other Spitfire and Hurricane squadrons operating in the same area.

On the 6th, Harker claimed two Bf 109s destroyed, both of which crashed near Eastbourne, plus two damaged, the kills being confirmed by Sqn.Ldr. J. S. O'Brien who also claimed two Bf 109s himself. Events on the 7th did not go so well for the squadron, although Sgt. Harker claimed another two Bf 109s plus another damaged. Confirmation was provided by P/O Robert Doe, 234 Squadron's top-scoring pilot and one of only 17 pilots with ten or more kills during the Battle of Britain. However, two of the squadron's pilots were lost including the CO, Sqn. Ldr. O'Brien. An odd entry which appears in Alan Harker's logbook for this day mentions that he attacked a '*German-flown Hurricane on P/O Doe's tail.*'

Sgt. Harker claimed another victory on 22 September, a dull and foggy day in which the *Luftwaffe* sent a Ju 88 from 4.(F)/121 to carry out a weather reconnaissance flight. Harker shot down this aircraft and saw it crash in flames into the sea 25 miles south-east of Land's End. Although his logbook states there were no survivors, the crew was in fact picked up by a trawler after ten hours in their dinghy. Harker claimed another Ju 88 damaged on 15 October. He was awarded the DFM on 22 October and was commissioned in March 1941.

At Warmwell on 1 April 1941, Harker was wounded in the arm during a low-level attack by He 111s, and on 19 May, he was shot down while carrying out a convoy patrol off Weymouth and crash-landed in a field near Warmwell.

On 4 August 1941, Harker was posted to 53 OTU at Llanlow as a Flight Commander, and from 27 June 1942, was a gunnery instructor at the Central Gunnery School at Sutton Bridge before moving to Llanbedr in December 1943 to form a Rocket Projectile School.

Posted to Italy on 5 July 1944, Harker then served as Motor Transport Officer with a mobile radar unit and was then Operations Officer with an American Liberator squadron and later a Polish squadron, both of which were engaged in supply-dropping operations. Released from the RAF as a Flight Lieutenant in November 1945, Alan Harker returned to civilian life and became a heating engineer. He died on 6 August 1996.

'I remember thinking of the injustice of it all . . .'

Flight Lieutenant Bob Oxspring flew Spitfires with No 66 Squadron during the Battle. Here he describes the action he is least likely to forget:

'25 October 1940; the Battle of Britain was in its closing stages, though at the time we had no way of knowing that this was the case. I was a very new Flight Lieutenant on No 66 Squadron, then based at Gravesend. Soon after breakfast we were scrambled and I was ordered to take my Flight of six Spitfires to patrol over Maidstone at 30,000 feet; the Germans were putting in the occasional fighter sweep and fighter-bomber attack and it was one of these we were after. When we arrived over Maidstone there was nothing to be seen, however; from the ground we received further orders to orbit overhead and wait.

'It was nearly half an hour later that the 'bandits' did show up: six Messerschmitt 109s. For once we had a perfect set-up: we were up-sun, we had a 2,000 foot drop on them and the numbers were exactly equal. It did not often turn out like that during the Battle of Britain. I told my pilots to take one each and down we went. But the Germans were wide awake and I watched my man, the leader, suddenly barrel round and pull his fighter into a steep dive. I had been half expecting it and I tore down after him almost vertically, gaining slowly but surely. I had him cold. It never occurred to me to watch my own tail – after all, we had covered all six of the Messerschmitts. Well, confidence is that nice warm feeling you have just before you slip over the banana skin. I was in range and just about to open fire when, suddenly, my Spitfire shuddered under the impact of a series of explosions. In fact those six Messerschmitts had been covering a seventh, a decoy aircraft a couple of thousand feet beneath them; their idea had been to bounce any of our fighters having a go at it. And the German leader had taken me right in front of the decoy, who got in a good squirt at me as I went past.

'He must have hit my elevator controls, because the next thing I knew my Spitfire was pulling uncontrollably up into a tight loop; a loop so tight that the 'G' forces squeezed me hard into my seat and blacked me out. As I went down the other side of the loop the aircraft straightened out and I could see again, but as the speed built up the jammed elevators took effect and up we went into a second loop. Obviously the time had come for me to part company with that Spitfire. But first I had to get the hood open and that was not proving easy: the only time I could reach up and see to do it was when the 'G' was off; but then we were screaming downhill fast and the hood would not budge. I thought my time had come and I remember thinking of the injustice of it all: hit just as I was about to blow that Messerschmitt out of the sky!

'I have no idea how many loops the Spitfire did before I was finally able to slide back the hood. But it was not a moment too soon, because by then the oil tank was on fire and the flames were spreading back from the engine. I threw off my seat harness and stood up, but found I could go no further because I still had my helmet

on and it was attached firmly to the aircraft. By now I was getting pretty desperate and I wrenched the helmet off with all my strength. Afterwards I found the helmet in the wreckage and saw that I had actually torn it across the leather; I was amazed at the force I must have summoned to do that.

'The next thing I knew I was falling clear of my aircraft, head-down and on my back, at an angle of about forty-five degrees. I had no idea how high I was, so I pulled the D-ring right away. I knew it was a mistake, as soon as I did it.

'When the parachute began to deploy, I was in just about the worst possible position. I remember watching, an interested spectator, as the canopy and the rigging lines came streaming out from between my legs. One of the lines coiled itself round my leg and when the canopy developed I found myself hanging upside down. I had never parachuted before, but from my sketchy previous instruction I was fairly certain that head-first was not the position to be in when I hit the ground! So I grabbed a handful of slack rigging lines on the opposite side to my entangled leg and started to climb up, hand-over-hand. After a lot of kicking and pulling, I managed to get my leg free; with a sigh of relief I sank back into my harness, right way up.

'Now I had time to think about what was happening around me. The first thing that struck me was the quietness; the only sounds were the spasmodic bursts of cannon and machine gun fire and the howls of the engines, coming from the battle still in progress high above; it seemed an age since I had been part of it. But my own troubles were not over yet.

'Gradually it began to dawn on me that the straps leading up from my harness, instead of being comfortably clear of my head on either side, were tangled together and chafing my ears and face. And higher up the rigging lines were also tangled, preventing the canopy from developing to its fullest extent. That meant that I was falling much faster than I should have been; and struggle as I might, I could not get the lines untangled. I went down past a cloud and it seemed to whiz by: it was not going to be a very pleasant landing. The only time I had ever needed a parachute and this had to happen!

'Gradually I got lower, and I could make out trees and farm houses and curious faces raised skywards. At about 500 feet the wind carried me across some high tension cables and even though I was hundreds of feet above the wires I could not resist the instinct to lift my feet up. Still I was coming down much too fast. The one thing I needed most of all was a nice soft tree, to break my fall. And there in my line of drift, in answer to my prayer, was a wood full of them.

'Just before I hit I covered my face with my arms and came to rest amid the crack of breaking twigs. When the noise stopped I cautiously lowered my arms and looked around. My parachute canopy was draped across a couple of trees and I was bouncing up and down between the trunks like a yo-yo. I was about twenty feet up, suspended above an asphalt road.

'At about my level, just out of reach, was a small branch. By doing a sort of Tarzan stunt, swinging back and forth from side to *side, I was able to get closer and closer until, in the end, I was able to grab hold of it. Gingerly I pulled myself up and on to a thicker bough, before letting go of my harness. By this time quite a crowd had begun to collect underneath the tree; at first there seemed to be some doubt about my nationality, but the vehemence of my Anglo-Saxon demands*

for help soon satisfied everyone that I was, in fact, British. Some Home Guard men made a human ladder by sitting on each others' shoulders and with their aid I managed to clamber down to mother earth. It had indeed been a memorable day.'

Sgt. Bohumir Furst, (Czechoslovakian), No. 310 Squadron

A total of 88 Czech volunteers served with the RAF during the Battle of Britain, at first being absorbed into Regular squadrons. Later, Fighter Command formed two special squadrons almost entirely composed of Czech personnel, the first, No. 310 Squadron, forming at Duxford on 10 July 1940. The squadron became operational on 18 August and its first combat occurred on 26 August when it claimed three enemy aircraft destroyed for the loss of three Hurricanes, the pilots of which were unhurt. No. 310 Squadron retained the code letters 'NN' until its repatriation to Czechoslovakia in 1946.

This photograph shows Sgt. Bohumir Furst who served with the pre-war Czech Air Force until the final German occupation in March 1939, at which time he escaped to join *l'Armée de 'Air* and, during the French campaign, shared in the destruction of an Hs 126 and the probable destruction of a Do 17. After the fall of France, Furst made his way to England and, in August 1940, was one of the first pilots to join the newly-formed 310 Squadron. During the Battle, Sgt. Furst claimed a Bf 110, a Bf 109 and an He 111. He was later commissioned, received the Czech Military Cross, and after leaving the RAF in 1946 as a Flight Lieutenant, returned to Czechoslovakia.

'D' Watch, WAAF plotters pictured outside the operations room at Biggin Hill.

Sgt. Josef Frantisek, (Czechoslovakian), No. 303 (Polish) Squadron

Josef Frantisek left his homeland in 1938 when the Germans occupied the Sudetenland – the western border of Czechoslovakia – and flew to Poland where he joined the Polish Air Force. Frantisek is believed to have shot down some German aircraft during the subsequent invasion of Poland in September 1939, and after it, escaped to Romania where he was interned. However, he escaped and via the Balkans and Syria, eventually arrived in France, just as the German invasion of that country began. Joining a French Air Force fighter squadron, Frantisek is believed to have destroyed 11 enemy aircraft, for which he was awarded the French *Croix de Guerre*.

When France fell, Frantisek escaped to England and joined 303 Squadron which was formed in July from Polish personnel evacuated from France, the squadron becoming operational soon afterwards with Hurricanes. Frantisek claimed his first kill of the Battle, a Bf 109, on 2 September and thereafter claimed regularly, sometimes destroying two aircraft on the same day, and on 11 September, he claimed two Bf 109s and an He 111. Not including claims made while flying with the French Air Force, his final total was 17 confirmed (six bombers, two Bf 110s and nine Bf 109s), making him the highest scorer of the Battle of Britain. This feat is all the more remarkable since it was achieved in less than a month, his last kill being a Bf 109 on 30 September. He was awarded the DFM by King George VI personally.

As with several other well-known flying personalities, Frantisek was killed not in combat but during a routine patrol, his Hurricane crashing at Ewell, Surrey, due to unknown causes on 20 September 1940, ironically just three days before 303 Sqn. was withdrawn to the quieter 12 Group area. He was posthumously awarded the Polish *Virtuti Militari* (5th Class), the *Krzyz Walecznych* and three Bars, and the Czech Military Cross.

Fuselage of a 303 Squadron Hurricane showing the Squadron badge, transferred from the Polish Air Force. The chalked number 126 refers to the number of enemy aircraft the squadron claimed destroyed.

NIGHT BLITZ AND TIP AND RUN - AIRCRAFT LOSSES

Note: On each night during this period, with the exception of that of 6 October when poor weather prevented operations, there was a large-scale attack on London. On some nights other cities were attacked also.

Date	Luftwaffe	RAF	Main Daylight Action
1 October	5	6	Fighter-bomber attacks on southern England.
2 October	15	1	Fighter sweeps over southern England.
3 October	7	1	Poor weather, little activity.
4 October	12	1	Poor weather, little activity.
5 October	12	5	Fighter-bomber attack on London.
6 October	5	2	Poor weather, little activity.
7 October	20	15	Attack on Yeovil.
8 October	12	3	Fighter-bomber attack on London.
9 October	8	2	Fighter-bomber attack on London.
10 October	5	6	Fighter-bomber attack on London.
11 October	7	9	Fighter-bomber attacks on south-east England.
12 October	12	9	Fighter-bomber attacks on south-east England.
13 October	4	2	Fighter-bomber attacks on south-east England.
14 October	3	1	Little activity.
15 October	8	12	Fighter-bomber attack on London.
16 October	12	1	Poor weather, little activity.
17 October	11	4	Fighter-bomber attack on London.
18 October	14	4	Poor weather, little activity.
19 October	2	0	Poor weather, little activity.
20 October	12	5	Fighter-bomber attack on London.
21 October	5	0	Poor weather, little activity.
22 October	10	6	Poor weather, little activity.
23 October	4	0	Poor weather, little activity.
24 October	6	1	Poor weather, little activity.
25 October	20	12	Fighter-bomber attacks on south-east England.
26 October	10	6	Fighter-bomber attacks on south-east England.
27 October	14	12	Fighter-bomber attacks on south-east England.
28 October	7	1	Attacks on shipping.
29 October	22	9	Fighter-bombers attacked London, Italian planes attacked Ramsgate.
30 October	7	7	Poor weather, little activity.
31 October	2	0	Poor weather, little activity.
1 November	4	9	Fighter-bomber attacks on SE England. Attack on shipping.
TOTALS	**297**	**152**	

THE BATTLE SUMMED UP CHAPTER 5

'A victory is very essential to England at the moment.'

ADMIRAL SIR JOHN JERVIS, AFTER THE BATTLE OF CAPE ST VINCENT, 1797

ADOLF HITLER conceded defeat in the Battle of Britain when, on 17 September, he ordered the planned invasion of southern England to be postponed until further notice. During the weeks that followed, the ships and barges concentrated at the Channel ports gradually dispersed, never to return.

During World War 2 three major battles signalled the end of the initial, defensive, phase of the conflict for the Allies: in the west, the Battle of Britain; in Russia, the halting of the German advance in front of Moscow; and in the Pacific, the loss of four Japanese aircraft carriers in a few hours during the Battle of Midway.

In each case, following a succession of disastrous military setbacks, Allied forces secured victories that stopped the Axis advance in its tracks and established a breathing space in which to build their strength before taking the offensive. The Battle of Britain was the first of those decisive battles and, arguably, it was the most important: had it not been won, the other battles might never have taken place. Or, if they had taken place, their outcome might have been different. That is the historical significance of the air battle fought over the south of England during the summer and autumn of 1940.

Although some air fighting took place before that time and some occurred after it, the major actions of the Battle of Britain all took place between 10 July and 1 November 1940. During that period the *Luftwaffe* lost 1,598 aircraft destroyed or damaged beyond repair, and the Royal Air Force lost 902 fighters. The overall ratio of losses throughout the Battle was 1.8: 1 in favour of the defenders.

Clearly the *Luftwaffe* lost the Battle of Britain but, it is pertinent to ask, could the Germans possibly have won it? Throughout the Battle, a primary aim of the *Luftwaffe* was the destruction of Royal Air Force Fighter Command as an effective fighting force. There were four methods available to the *Luftwaffe* for achieving this: by the destruction of fighters in the air; by the destruction of fighter airfields and fighters on the ground; by the destruction of the fighter control system, including the radar stations; and by the destruction of factories producing the fighters.

The German tactics of sending escorted formations of bombers to attack targets in southern England were successful in forcing the RAF fighter squadrons to do battle; but in the combats that followed, the German fighter force was unable to establish any lasting degree of air superiority or inflict decisively heavy losses on the defenders.

Nor did the attacks on airfields weaken Fighter Command to any significant extent. Although all of No 11 Group's main sector airfields, at Tangmere, Kenley, Biggin Hill, Hornchurch and North Weald, were hit hard, none was put out of action for more than a few hours. With the general purpose bombs available to the *Luftwaffe*, it was almost impossible to crater a grass airfield so severely that no clear strip 700 yards long remained from which

Hurricanes of No 615 Squadron pictured after landing at Northolt in October 1940. At that stage in the Battle the Luftwaffe had given up attacking Fighter Command airfields, and there was no need to disperse the fighters for protection.

A Bf 109 E-1 of 7./JG 54 lies on the shingle on a beach near Lydd, in Kent, after its pilot, Uffz. Arno Zimmermann put it down after sustaining damage to his engine following a dogfight with Hurricanes of 605 Squadron on 27 October 1940.

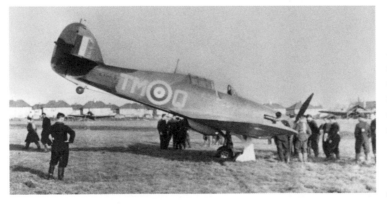

As summer turned to autumn, a greater proportion of missions were flown at night and in poor weather, and both sides lost numerous aircraft in flying accidents. This Hurricane of No 504 Squadron tipped on to its nose after running into soft ground at Filton in October.

What might have been: German troops landing somewhere on the south coast during Operation Sealion? Actually, no: these troops are seen in training on the French coast.

An important part of Britain's defence on home soil was the Home Guard – (initially known as 'Local Defence Volunteers', or in slang, 'Look-Duck-Vanish', it was later referred to affectionately as 'Dad's Army'). Operational from 1940 until 1944, and comprising 1.5 million local volunteers otherwise ineligible for military service, usually owing to age, the Home Guard acted as a secondary defence force, in case of invasion.

The part played by 'Ultra' during the Battle of Britain

Since the success of the British 'Ultra' cipher-breaking operation at Bletchley Park was officially revealed, there have been questions regarding the use of this information in the tactical handling of Fighter Command during the Battle of Britain. In spite of a careful search of the archives and close questioning of those interviewed, the author has found no hard evidence to support that view. Certainly Ultra provided much useful intelligence on the *Luftwaffe* during the summer of 1940, but the information was usually fragmentary and rarely was it of immediate use to RAF Fighter Command. During the Battle of Britain most *Luftwaffe* signals traffic was sent by landline, and this traffic could not be picked up by British listening posts. Relatively little traffic relating to the Battle was passed by wireless, and only a small proportion of that was decrypted and read by British Intelligence in 1940.

Often the information received via Ultra was too vague to be of operational value. For example, between 9 and 13 August, several decrypted signals referred to '*Adlertag*' ('Eagle Day'). But neither the code-breakers at Bletchley Park, nor Air Intelligence could discover the exact meaning of that code-word although, obviously, it referred to a major operation in the offing. Only after the operation was launched did it become clear that '*Adlertag*' referred to the first day in a series of large-scale attacks on airfields in the south of England.

There were other limitations on the value of Ultra information that prevented its use in tactical situations. Although the code-breakers sometimes provided advance notice of the timing and the forces committed to attack individual targets, the *Luftwaffe* referred to the latter by their serial number in its catalogue of targets. For example, Kenley airfield was Target No 10118, and Northolt airfield was Target No 10160. The meaning of individual target numbers would become known to RAF Intelligence only over a long period, and throughout the Battle of Britain the meanings of most of these numbers was not known.

Also, the *Luftwaffe* often made last-minute alterations of its attack plans, to take into account the predicted weather or other factors. Often these changes were not picked up at Bletchley Park. For example, on 14 September decrypts revealed that a large-scale attack was to take place against London, and they listed the units to take part. But previous decrypts had announced that the raid was scheduled for the afternoon of 13 September, and it did not take place. The raid was finally launched on 15 September, with no further warning from Ultra.

During the Battle of Britain, the first reliable indication of the approach of raiding forces came when those forces appeared on radar. And it was on this information, and not that from Ultra, that the defending fighters were deployed.

fighters could operate. In any case, craters could quickly be filled with rubble and rolled flat, and each station had an efficient organisation to do that. Only one Fighter Command airfield was put out of action for any length of time and that one, Manston, was not one of the all-important sector stations.

The attacks on airfields failed to destroy fighters on the ground in significant numbers to be decisive – squadrons at high states of readiness were usually airborne and clear of their base long before an attack could develop. Between 13 August and 6 September airfields in southern England were attacked on almost every day that the weather allowed. But less than a score of fighters belonging to front-line units were destroyed on the ground.

Some commentators have suggested that had the *Luftwaffe* continued its attack on the radar stations along the south coast of England, these vital installations could have been knocked out. That could have deprived Fighter Command of the early warning necessary for its squadrons to go into action effectively. But the radar stations were small pinpoint targets, not easy to hit from the air. Moreover, damage to the radar equipments could usually be repaired quickly. And where this was not the case Fighter Command possessed mobile reserve equipments that could be moved in rapidly to plug the gaps in the radar cover. Although several radar stations were attacked and damaged, only one (that at Ventnor on the Isle of Wight) remained out of action for more than a few hours.

Finally, as a means of reducing the effectiveness of Fighter Command, the *Luftwaffe* could attack the factories producing the fighter airframes and engines. Spitfire production was centred at Woolston, Itchen and Eastleigh near Southampton, with production building up at the new plant at Castle Bromwich near Birmingham. Hurricanes were produced at Langley, Brooklands and Kingston in Surrey, and at Brockworth in Gloucestershire. The Merlin engines that powered these fighters were built at the Rolls-Royce plants at Derby, Crewe and Glasgow. Scores of factories throughout the country acted as sub-contractors, however, producing components for these fighters and their engines.

The *Luftwaffe* could certainly have done more against the factories producing fighters, especially those around Southampton and in Surrey that could be reached by escorted bomber formations. Yet, as we have seen, when the factories at Woolston and Itchen were bombed successfully, it took only a few weeks to disperse production of Spitfires into the surrounding area and resume it there. Once dispersed in this way, aircraft production facilities were almost invulnerable to air attack.

At no time did the combined attacks on RAF Fighter Command seriously weaken the force. Throughout the battle the Command possessed an average of fifty squadrons with a total of just over one thousand fighters; of that thousand, about 720 fighters were available for operations on any one day. Although there were shortfalls from time to time, in general the manufacture and repair of fighters kept pace with RAF losses. Thus, at the beginning of October 1940, Fighter Command was numerically as strong as it had been at the beginning of August.

Much has been said of the losses in pilots suffered by Fighter Command, and these were indeed serious. But the *Luftwaffe* suffered serious losses in trained personnel also. During the large-scale actions, for each RAF pilot killed or wounded, it cost the *Luftwaffe* five or more aircrew killed, wounded or taken prisoner. The ratio of 5: 1 was close to that between the number of German aircrew involved in the Battle, and those in Fighter Command. In other words, the two sides suffered similar losses in trained aircrew, in proportion to their overall strengths. Had it persisted in its attempts to smash Fighter Command, the *Luftwaffe* was likely to smash itself also.

Given the quality of the leadership, the training and the equipment of Fighter Command and the high morale of its personnel, given the ability of the British aircraft industry to build and repair fighters in sufficient numbers, given the resilience of the British people in the face of air attack and finally – and probably most important of all – given the ability of Prime Minister Winston Churchill to rouse the nation to action, given these factors the *Luftwaffe* could never have won the Battle. And it does no discredit to 'The Few' to say so.

32 Squadron Hurricane pilots relax at readiness at Biggin Hill, with one of the unit's Hurricanes, GZ-V, behind. Peter Malam ('Pete') Brothers, a well known ace, is seen fourth from left.

Appendix A

Equivalent ranks: *Luftwaffe*, Royal Air Force, US Army Air Forces

Luftwaffe	Royal Air Force	USAAF
Generalfeldmarschall	Marshal of the R.A.F.	(no equivalent)
Generaloberst	Air Chief Marshal	General (4 star)
General der Flieger	Air Marshal	General (3 star)
Generalleutnant	Air Vice-Marshal	General (2 star)
Generalmajor	Air Commodore	General (1 star)
Oberst	Group Captain	Colonel
Oberstleutnant	Wing Commander	Lieutenant Colonel
Major	Squadron Leader	Major
Hauptmann	Flight Lieutenant	Captain
Oberleutnant	Flying Officer	1st Lieutenant
Leutnant	Pilot Officer	2nd Lieutenant
Stabsfeldwebel	Warrant Officer	Warrant Officer
Oberfeldwebel	Flight Sergeant	Master Sergeant
Feldwebel	Sergeant	Technical Sergeant
Unterfeldwebel	(no equivalent)	(no equivalent)
Unteroffizier	Corporal	Staff Sergeant
Hauptgefreiter	(no equivalent)	Sergeant
Obergefreiter	Leading Aircraftman	Corporal
Gefreiter	Aircraftman First Class	Private First Class
Flieger	Aircraftman Second Class	Private Second

Appendix B

LUFTWAFFE FLYING UNITS

The *Staffel*

During the Battle of Britain the *Staffel* (plural *Staffeln*) had a nominal strength of nine aircraft, and it was the smallest combat flying unit generally use in the *Luftwaffe*. The *Staffeln* within a *Geschwader* were designated using Arabic numbers. Thus the 1., 2. and 3. *Staffeln* belonged to the I. *Gruppe*. The 4., 5. and 6. belonged to the II. *Gruppe* and 7., 8. and 9. *Staffeln* belonged to the III. *Gruppe*.

The *Gruppe*

The *Gruppe* (plural *Gruppen*) was the basic flying unit of the *Luftwaffe* for operational and administrative purposes. Initially it was established at three *Staffeln* each with nine aircraft, plus a Staff Flight with three, making 30 aircraft in all. After a prolonged period in action a *Gruppe* could be considerably smaller than that, however.

The *Geschwader*

The *Geschwader* (plural *Geschwader*) was the largest flying unit in the *Luftwaffe* to have a fixed nominal strength, initially three *Gruppen* with a total of 90 aircraft, and a Staff unit of four, making a total of 94 aircraft. Originally it had been intended that the *Gruppen* of each *Geschwader* would operate from adjacent airfields, but under the stress of war this idea soon had to be abandoned.

The *Fliegerkorps* and the *Luftflotte*
The *Fliegerkorps* (Air Corps) and the larger *Luftflotte* (Air Fleet) varied in size, and the number of *Gruppen* assigned to them depended on the importance of their particular area of operations.

Appendix C

LUFTWAFFE UNIT ROLE PREFIXES

The main *Geschwader*, *Gruppen* and *Staffeln* prefixes (abbreviated prefixes in brackets) to denote their operational roles were as follows:

Aufklärungs- (Aufkl.)	Reconnaissance
Erprobungs- (Erpr.)	Operational Trials Unit
Fernaufklärungs- (FA)	Long Range Reconnaissance
Jagd- (J)	Fighter
Jagdbomber- (Jabo)	Fighter-Bomber
Kampf- (K)	Bomber
Küstenflieger- (Kü.Fl)	Unit engaged in coastal operations.
Lehr- (L)	Tactical Development Unit
Sturzkampf- (St)	Dive bomber
Wettererkundungs- (Weku)	Weather Reconnaissance
Zerstörer- (Z)	Twin-engined fighter ('destroyer')

Appendix D

RAF Fighter Command Tactical Memorandum No. 8, June 1940
This secret document, excerpts of which are reproduced below, was circulated throughout RAF fighter units in June 1940 and reflected the current state of tactical thinking. The memorandum remained in force until November 1940, when revised instructions were issued [*the author's comments, where applicable, are in italics in square brackets.*]

```
Introduction
German tactics during the present phase have shown that, in large scale
attacks, bombers are invariably escorted by formations of fighters, whose
duty it is to protect them from our fighters.

    The German Air Force has now established bases in Norway, Holland,
Belgium and Northern France. Southern and South-Eastern England are now
within the effective range of the Me 109, and the Me 110 can cover the whole
of England and Scotland.

    Our fighters have been taking a heavy toll of both these types under the
more difficult conditions of the past few weeks, and results have shown
that the Hurricane and Spitfire are more than a match for either the Me 109
or the Me 110. Under conditions of Home Defence, where a highly organised
system exists, the task of our Air Force should be simplified. Already we
have established a very definite moral ascendancy over the enemy, who are
unwilling to stay and fight unless in superior numbers.
```
[*That last sentence would certainly not be borne out during the initial phases of the Battle of Britain*].

The Aim

It may here be clearly stated that our ability to continue the war rests to a very large extent on the success of our fighters, in conjunction with the Fixed Defences, in the protection of our vital centres, and especially those concerned with aircraft.

It must, therefore, be constantly borne in mind that our aim is THE DESTRUCTION OF ENEMY BOMBERS, and that action against fighters is only a means to this end.

A study of enemy tactics which will probably be employed is therefore necessary so that the best means of achieving this aim can be put into effect.

German tactics

Bombers usually approach their objectives in sub-formations in line astern, each sub-formation consisting of three, five, or seven aircraft in 'Vic', so disposed that they are mutually supporting. Large formations in several columns, staggered laterally and vertically have also been encountered and other formations may be developed.

The escorting fighters are normally between two and four thousand feet above and usually in the rear of the formation. Where two or more escorting Squadrons are employed they are normally in Squadron formation, with Squadrons stepped up to the rear and echeloned to one side or the other. These fighters frequently remain in position until our fighters attempt to attack the bombers. They then attack in a dive when our fighters' attention is taken up with their targets. This form of attack consists of a straight dive by individual fighters, the dive being continued well below. They then return, if numerically superior, and continue the same tactics.

It has been found that, owing to a healthy respect for our eight-gun fighters, enemy fighter formations will usually break up when attacked. [*When the German fighters entered a crossover turn, to watching RAF pilots it would have looked as though they were breaking formation.*] It is therefore essential to neutralise them with a part of our force, so that the remainder may deliver their attack on the bombers without interference. This is discussed more fully in the following paragraphs, which deal with our tactics.

THE ATTACK OF ESCORTED FORMATIONS

Search

Fighters in search formation should always patrol higher than the anticipated or reported heights of the enemy if weather conditions permit. It should be a fundamental principle that the rear units of any formation should be employed solely on look-out duties to avoid any possibility of surprise from astern or above.

Thus the essential 'Upper guard' is supplied, not only in that the second Squadron acts as such, but the rear Section of each Squadron supplies this cover to its own unit. Whatever the strength of the fighter unit, a proportion of it should always be detailed for this duty.

Approach

Upon approaching the enemy bombers, every effort should be made to achieve surprise. If this is successful it may be possible to deliver an attack without interference. The 'Upper' Squadron or Unit may be able to draw off their escort and, if necessary, attack them while the 'Lower' Squadron attacks the bombers. Remembering that the escorts are primarily fixed gun fighters, even a small detachment from our fighters, by attacking one after the other of the enemy fighters quickly from above, without getting closely engaged, may draw large numbers of them off and so enable the remaining fighters to deliver an attack unmolested.

Should our fighter formation be weak in comparison with the enemy's, the guard aircraft may have to be content with engaging their attention as much as possible and warning the fighters attacking the enemy bombers by R/T, when the enemy fighters move in to attack.

Always ensure that the upper guard is in position ready to assist before attacking, or that the enemy has no available protection.

The Attack

Whenever possible, fighters should attack enemy bomber formations in equal numbers by astern or quarter attacks from the same level, taking care not to cut the corners while closing in to decisive range, and thus presenting a side view target to the bombers' rear guns. They should keep their nose on the enemy and then, when at decisive range, make a deflection shot if required. If in a good position, a short burst of two or three seconds may well be decisive, but in any case this should not be exceeded without breaking away to ensure that an enemy fighter is not on one's tail. If all is well, the attack can be immediately renewed.

Whenever fighters that are attacking bombers receive warning from their upper guard of an impending attack by enemy fighters, they should immediately break away outwards. The German fighters frequently dive once in such an attack, and carry on away from the combat.

Should the fighters not be numerically strong enough to engage the enemy bombers aircraft for aircraft, it will be necessary to 'nibble' from the flanks. Fighters should be most careful not to approach into the 'Vic' of the bomber formation, as this will expose them to effective cross fire.

Breakaway

Fighter aircraft, when breaking away from a bomber formation, should endeavour to maintain the maximum relative speed. A steep and violent climbing turn results in the air gunner being given a period in which the only relative movement between himself and the fighter is that of an extension of range, and therefore he has practically a point-blank aim at the fighters.

The best form of breakaway would appear to be a downward turn, thus keeping up maximum speed and gradually changing the angle of flight paths of the bomber and the fighter.

FIGHTERS V. FIGHTERS

It is probable that the enemy will operate independent fighter formations over this country for the purpose of:

(i) Gaining air superiority.

(ii) Carrying out low attacks on aerodromes and dispersed aircraft.

(iii) Attempting to draw off our fighters prior to bombing attacks, whilst our fighters are re-fuelling and rearming (this latter practice has been frequently carried out in France).

The allocation of forces will be decided by the Group or Sector Commander, but fighter units should always remember that to waste petrol and ammunition under these circumstances may well be playing into the hands of the enemy. It may be necessary, therefore, for our fighters to adopt a purely defensive role for the protection of the aerodrome, and not attack these fighters, who are in the nature of a decoy, so that when the bombing forces arrive they will be able to attack them and shoot them down.

When battle is engaged with fighters, a dog-fight nearly always ensues. It may be a matter of individual combat, but whenever possible fighters should remain together so that they may afford mutual support.

When a fighter unit is attacking enemy fighters, Sections should be led into the attack together. As already stated, such attacks must invariably develop into a series of dog-fights and whenever possible our fighters should attempt to remain loosely in Section formation, or at least in pairs, so as to afford mutual support and to assist in the reformation of the unit after combat. On no account should individual fighters leave a formation to deliver attacks unless specifically ordered to do so.

SUMMARY

The following points are again emphasized:

(i)   It is essential that leaders should weigh up the situation as a whole before delivering attacks. Rushing blindly in to attack an enemy may have disastrous results, and will certainly be less effective.

(ii)   Never fly straight, either in the formation as a whole or individually. When over enemy territory alter course and height with a view to misleading AA. [anti-aircraft guns].

(iii)   Keep a constant watch to the rear of the formation of aircraft.

(iv)   Upon hearing close gun fire, turn immediately. Hesitancy in so doing may result in effective enemy fire. Do not dive straight away.

(v)   Before taking off, search the sky for enemy fighters, and if they are known to be about, turn as soon as possible after taking off. Enemy fighters have frequently dived on aircraft whilst they were taking off from their aerodromes. Similar remarks apply during approach and landing.

(vi)   Conserve ammunition as much as possible. A short burst at effective range is usually decisive, and leaves further ammunition for further attacks.

(vii) Exploit surprise to the utmost. The enemy has been taught to do this, and you should be prepared accordingly.

(viii) Always remember that your objective is the ENEMY BOMBER."

Further Reading

Note: works marked ★ are in German

★Balke, Ulf, *Kampfgeschwader 100,* Motorbuch Verlag, Stuttgart.

Barclay, George, *Angels 22,* Arrow Books, London.

Barker, E. C., *The Fighter Aces of the R.A.F.,* William Kimber, London.

Bekker, Cajus, *The Luftwaffe War Diaries,* Macdonald, London.

Bickers, Richard Townsend, *Ginger Lacey, Fighter Pilot,* Robert Hale, London.

Bishop, Edward, *Their Finest Hour,* Ballantine, New York.

Boorman, H.R.P., *Hell's Corner 1940,* Kent Messenger, Maidstone.

Brickhill, Paul, *Reach for the Sky,* Collins, London.

★Brütting, Georg, *Das waren die Deutschen Kampfflieger Asse 1939-1945,* Motorbuch Verlag, Stuttgart.

Bungay, Steven, *Most Dangerous Enemy,* Aurum.

Carne, Daphne, *The Eyes of the Few,* Macmillan, London.

Collier, Basil, *The Defence of the United Kingdom,* HMSO, London.

Collier, Richard, *Eagle Day,* Hodder and Stoughton, London.

Churchill, Winston, *The Second World War,* Volume 2, Cassell, London.

★Dierich, Wolfgang, *Die Verbände der Luftwaffe 1935-1945* Motorbuch Verlag, Stuttgart.
    — ★*Kampfgeschwader 55,* Motorbuch Verlag, Stuttgart.

Forrester, Larry, *Fly For Your Life,* Frederick Muller, London.

Galland, Adolf, *The First and the Last,* Methuen, London.

Green, William, *Warplanes of the Third Reich,* Macdonald and Jane's, London.

★Gundelach, Karl, *Kampfgeschwader 4,* Motorbuch Verlag, Stuttgart.

Hinsley, F.W., *British Intelligence in the Second World War,* HMSO, London, 1979.

HMSO Official Publications (authors not named)
    — *Front Line,* 1940-41. The story of Civil Defence.
    — *Roof Over Britain; the Story of the AA Defences.*
    — *The Battle of Britain.*

★Kiehl, Heinz, *Kampfgeschwader 53,* Motorbuch Verlag, Stuttgart.

Mason, Francis, *Battle over Britain,* McWhirter Twins, London.

McKee, Alexander, *Strike from the Sky,* Souvenir Press, London.

Neil, *Gun Button to Fire,* William Kimber Ltd, London.

★Obermaier, Ernst, *Die Ritterkreuzträger der Luftwaffe, Jagdflieger 1939-45,* Verlag Diether Hoffmann, Mainz.

Price, Alfred, *Battle of Britain, The Hardest Day,* Arms and Armour Press, London.
    — *Battle of Britain Day, 15 September 1940,* Arms and Armour Press, London.
    — *Blitz on Britain,* Ian Allan, Shepperton.
    — *Luftwaffe Handbook,* Ian Allan, Shepperton.
    — *The Bomber in World War II,* Arms and Armour Press, London.
    — *The Spitfire Story,* Arms and Armour Press, London.
    — *World War II Fighter Conflict,* Arms and Armour Press, London. Ramsey, Winston, et al.

The Battle of Britain, Then And Now, After the Battle, London.

Rawlings, John, *Fighter Squadrons of the R.A.F.,* Macdonald and Jane's, London.

Shores, Christopher, and Williams, Clive, *Aces High,* Grub Street.

Woods, Derek, and Dempster, Derek, *The Narrow Margin,* Hutchinson, London.

Wright, Robert, *Dowding and the Battle of Britain,* Macdonald and Jane's, London.

Pilots' Diaries:

Crossley, Michael, No 32 Squadron

Marrs, Eric, No 152 Squadron

Archive Sources

Air Ministry, *Air Defence of the United Kingdom*, copy held in the UK National Archives, Kew. Pilots' Combat Reports, Fighter Command, Group and station records, Anti-Aircraft Command records, Home Office bomb damage records, records held in UK National Archives, Kew.

Various records at the Bundesarchiv Militärarchiv, Freiburg-im-Breisgau.

As the air fighting tapered off, there was time to relax after the previous weeks' exertions. The scenes on this page were taken at No 504 Squadron then based at Filton. Here Pilot Officers Trevor Parsons (left) and Tony Rook wait at readiness.

High jinks among the Squadron's sergeant pilots, with H. Jones on the left and 'Wag' Haw on the right.

'Suzie', the Squadron's bulldog mascot.